The Doomsday Prepping
Crash Course

The Doomsday Prepping Crash Course

The Ultimate Prepper's Guide to Getting Prepared When You're on a Tight Budget

By Patty Hahne

SKYHORSE PUBLISHING

Skyhorse Publishing books may be purchased in bulk at special discounts for sales promotion, corporate gifts, fund-raising, or educational purposes. Special editions can also be created to specifications. For details, contact the Special Sales Department, Skyhorse Publishing, 307 West 36th Street, 11th Floor, New York, NY 10018 or info@ skyhorsepublishing.com.

Skyhorse® and Skyhorse Publishing® are registered trademarks of Skyhorse Publishing, Inc.®, a Delaware corporation.

www.skyhorsepublishing.com

10 9 8 7 6 5 4 3 2 1

Library of Congress Cataloging-in-Publication Data is available on file.

ISBN: 978-1-62087-874-3

Printed in the United States of America

DISCLAIMER

The purpose of this book is to help people with their emergency preparedness plans. It's the goal of this author to provide the most accurate information possible. The author believes, to the best of her knowledge, that the information provided in this book is correct at the time of this writing.

The author of this book provides tips about the types of items that she feels should be packed in a "bug out" bag. These tips are not all inclusive and you should pack your bug out bag or survival kit according to what you personally need to survive with as your needs may be different than hers.

Some items that the author suggests including in bug out bags may present a danger to young children. Before placing any of the items outlined in this book in a child's bug out bag, you should decide for yourself if you think it will be safe for your child to handle and use the item. Only you know the level of maturity of your children and you alone bear the burden of making sure that dangerous items are not packed in your children's bug out bags.

The information contained herein is intended for informational purposes only and the author claims no liability for the use or misuse of anything contained in this book. Any trademarks mentioned in this book are done so only for editorial purposes. These trademarks are the property of their respective owners and the author of this book is not affiliated with them in any way.

CONTENTS

Section 1

The Doomsday Prepping Crash Course

Introduction

There are a growing number of people who proudly call themselves "preppers" in the world today. A prepper is someone who spends their time preparing for what is commonly called "doomsday." In this day and age, the prepper community is one that is growing by leaps and bounds. It's a subculture of people who see the importance of preparing for the harsh times that are to come.

People from all walks of life are feeling a sense of urgency to prepare for some form of a doomsday-type event that is bound to happen sooner or later. Whether it will be a catastrophic natural disaster, an economic crisis caused by hyperinflation, or some other kind of major event, one thing is certain: Those who have prepared will have a much better chance of weathering the storm than those who did not take the time to do so.

It's no secret that the US economy has seen better days. With the unemployment rate above 8 percent, many people are finding it a bit tough to stretch their money and make it from paycheck to paycheck. If people are having a hard time finding enough money to pay the bills, how on earth can they find the money to prepare to survive a major natural or economic disaster? Luckily, this book will teach you some helpful tips that you can use to prepare for doomsday—even if you're on a tight budget.

In the following pages, you'll find tips and tricks that you can use to save money while prepping, in addition to useful advice to help you understand the kinds of preparations you should be making and the types of items you should be stockpiling.

The First Step in Prepping Is the Most Important

The single most important step to prepping is to simply start doing it. This may seem easier said than done if you are on a tight budget, but it's the truth. The most important and difficult thing for people to do is to just get started doing something.

Many people tend to feel so overwhelmed with the huge list of things that should be done to prepare for a doomsday event that they never actually take any steps to get started. Looking at prepping like this is backwards

thinking. It's extremely important that you break prepping down to its individual components and tackle them one by one. Remember that old saying that says the way to eat an elephant is one bite at a time? This is especially true when it comes to prepping.

Even the preppers with the most impressive stockpiles and plans started somewhere. Do you know where they started? They all started at the beginning, just like you will. It's true that some people have more money and resources than others, but everyone started somewhere.

There are plenty of wealthy individuals who haven't spent a single cent prepping despite the fact that they have unlimited resources. Likewise, there are plenty of people who barely get by from month-to-month who have a rather impressive stockpile of supplies and well-thought-out and designed emergency preparedness plans.

As you are reading through this book, try to keep things in perspective. You may end up choosing to adopt some of the advice that is given in this book and ignore other parts of it altogether. Remember that prepping is a process and it's one that most preppers never actually complete. We're constantly prepping and doing the things that we think will help us survive doomsday.

The bottom line is that doing something to prepare is much better than doing nothing at all. Some of you will choose to only do a few things that are outlined in this book. Others will go to the extreme end of the spectrum and do much more. The important thing is that you do something—and the goal of this book is to help you do just that!

Getting Your Priorities Straight from the Beginning

One thing that all good preppers have in common is that they have their priorities straight. They have all come to a point in their lives that has enabled them to make a real commitment to prepping. It's one thing to say that you would like to start prepping, but it's something entirely different to actually make a serious commitment to start and stick with it.

If you really want to be a prepper, you need to make a commitment to prepping. If you're on a budget, this will likely mean that you'll have to make some personal sacrifices. You'll need to take a close look at how you spend your money and find ways to free up money to buy prepping supplies.

 Now, before you say that there's just no money in your budget to start prepping, you really should challenge yourself to take a good, close look at your budget and do an "honest" evaluation. You may need to be brutally honest with yourself and ask some tough questions.

For example, if you think that it's impossible to start your day without stopping by your favorite coffee shop for a grande low-fat latte with a double shot of espresso, you're probably not being honest with yourself.

These are the types of things that people can cut out of their budget to free up money that can be spent on prepping. Let's take a closer look at this example. If you spend $3 a day for your gourmet coffee, that's $1,080 that you're spending each year just to feed your morning coffee habit. This doesn't even include how much you spend in gas to make a special trip to the coffee shop every day!

Drinking gourmet coffee may not be your particular vice, but if you take a good look at your budget, you'll probably

find something that can be eliminated—or at the very least, cut back on. Maybe you'll have to cancel your $100/month satellite TV subscription. That would free up $1,200 a year that you could spend on prepping supplies. Maybe you can trade in your huge four-wheel drive Suburban for a gas-saving economy car. You could then use the money that you save on gas for prepping.

The point is that most people aren't really being honest with themselves when they say that there just isn't any room in the budget to start prepping. In most cases, with a little creative thinking, you can find some money to allocate to the prepping portion of your budget. It often really just depends on how badly you actually *want* to start prepping.

Having Good Plans in Place Will Pave the Way to Success

Soon we'll get into the meat and potatoes of this book and share some great prepping tips, but before we do that, let's talk about the importance of having good prepping plans in place.

It's very easy to get overwhelmed with everything that need to be done to successfully prepare for doomsday. Being overwhelmed will either lead to frantic unorganized prepping or doing nothing at all to prepare. Neither of these are good paths to take.

The best advice for now is to read through this book entirely. This will help you become familiar with the tasks that need to be done to prepare for doomsday. Then, take an afternoon to sit down and write a list of all the things you would like to do to prepare for doomsday. Write this list as if you had the money to go out and buy everything today. This will help make sure that you're not leaving items out because you're worried about how much everything will cost.

Once you have this list made out, it's time to break the list down into things that you can do right away. There will be plenty that you can do to prepare that won't cost much, if any, money at all. The simple fact that you are doing something to prepare will motivate you and inspire you to continue prepping. That's why it's so important to get started doing the little inexpensive things right away.

Next write down your mid-term goals and your long-term goals, being sure to include the dates that you would like to accomplish them. Don't be afraid to set goals because they are, in fact, only goals. If you have to adjust the dates later on down the road, that's just fine. The important thing to remember is that you are more likely to achieve goals you have written down than those you haven't written down.

You're going to want to have a few different types of plans in place. The first is the plan that includes the list

of tangible items that you'll need to collect to put away in your emergency supplies cache. We'll cover these later on in this book.

The second type of plan includes the intangible things that you should be doing to prepare for doomsday. These include increasing your knowledge, skills, and physical fitness so that when you eventually find yourself having to survive in a crisis, you'll be up for the challenge. We'll cover these topics later in this book, as well.

The third type of plan that you should have in place is your "bug out" plan. A bug out plan is ideal and necessary for times when it might become too dangerous to stay in your home. Depending upon where you live, you may plan to try to stay put and survive at home for as long as you can. In the prepping world, people call this "bugging in."

Regardless of how well you plan and prepare to bug in, you need to be prepared to get out of town if conditions become too dangerous at home. When it comes to bugging out, you should try to anticipate multiple scenarios, which means that you should have several evacuation routes in mind. If you only have one planned evacuation route in mind and half a million other people happen to have the *same* idea, you'll find yourself wishing

you had taken the time to include multiple evacuation routes in your planning.

Having these three types of plans in place will enable you to move forward as you prepare for doomsday and

achieve your goals one by one. If you try to be a prepper without having well-thought-out plans in place, you'll find yourself wandering aimlessly as you gather a little here and there. Ultimately, you won't end up being nearly as prepared as you would have been if you had followed a set of detailed plans.

Avoid Frustration by Starting With the Easy Things First

When getting started as a prepper, it's easy to focus too much on the "cool prepping gear." You might spend your time some days dreaming about that 2,000-square-foot underground survival bunker that you've always wanted to build.

You may even fool yourself into believing that you're actually prepping by spending countless hours designing every last detail of your ideal emergency bunker. The reality is that you're not really doing anything to prepare unless you actually have the funds to follow through and install and build the bunker. If you don't have the money to follow through with this project, you're just daydreaming and wasting time. Instead of daydreaming about prepping, you should spend your time actually *doing* something that will help you survive when doomsday finally arrives.

A great example of an easy way to get started is storing water. As a matter of fact, one of the most important elements of any prepper's stockpile should be their water supply. Ironically, storing water is one of the least expensive and easiest things a prepper can do.

The main thing to keep in mind is that doing something is always better than doing nothing when it comes to prepping. Putting up water may not be as fun as dreaming up all the cool features that you would like to have in your ideal emergency bunker, but it needs to be done. And, best of all, it doesn't cost much money to do.

Properly Storing Water for Emergency Use

Did you know that, according to the Federal Emergency Management Agency (FEMA), the average adult should store at least one half gallon of water to be used solely for drinking for each day that they won't have access to a safe water supply? They actually advise us all to store at least one gallon of water per person per day.

Some preppers have huge water cisterns they use to store thousands of gallons of water, but most preppers either can't afford to or aren't equipped to store this much water. The good news is that virtually anyone can start storing water while recycling at the same time.

In a document that FEMA has provided to teach people about storing water (www.ready.gov/water), they suggest using empty two-liter soda bottles to store water. Two of these bottles hold the equivalent of 1.056 gallons of water. Based on FEMA's recommendation of storing one gallon of water per person per day, two two-liter soda

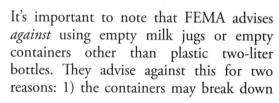

bottles filled with clean water would be adequate to meet the average person's daily water requirements.

It's important to note that FEMA advises *against* using empty milk jugs or empty containers other than plastic two-liter bottles. They advise against this for two reasons: 1) the containers may break down and start leaking, and 2) it isn't possible to adequately sterilize the containers for safe water storage.

The process for storing water in empty two-liter bottles is quite simple. Wash the inside of the empty bottle with dishwashing soap and water, making sure to thoroughly rinse out any soap residue. You should then sanitize the bottle by adding a teaspoon of regular nonscented liquid household chlorine bleach and one quart of regular tap water to the empty bottle. (Don't use any bleach that has any additives in it.) Shake the bottle thoroughly and then pour out the sanitizing solution and rinse the bottle with clean tap water. Don't forget to sanitize the cap while you're sanitizing the bottle.

Don't use empty milk containers for storing water.

Now that you have a freshly sanitized bottle, simply fill it with regular tap water. Please note that if the water

from your tap is treated with chlorine at a commercial water treatment plant, there's no need to treat the water further. You can use it straight from the tap as is. If, however, your tap water hasn't been commercially treated, you should add two drops of nonscented liquid household chlorine bleach to the bottle after you have filled it.

Next, tightly seal the bottle with the freshly sanitized cap, careful not to touch the inside of the cap with your finger, which could contaminate the water. FEMA says that you can store water like this for up to six months if you keep it stored in a cool, dark place. Be sure and write with a permanent marker on the bottle the date that you filled it so you'll know when to replace the water. It would also be a good idea to write the expiration date on the bottle, as well. Before the expiration date arrives, you should rotate the old water out and replace it with fresh water.

Money Saving Tip: If you already drink soda, you can switch to buying it in two-liter bottles instead of cans and start stocking up on water by filling the empty bottles. If you don't drink soda, you can probably find some friends or coworkers who will save their empty bottles and give them to you. This is a great way to acquire empty bottles for storing water and it won't cost you a single penny!

Note: The one gallon of water per person per day suggestion is just a recommendation. Depending on the temperature, the level of physical activity, the health of the individual, and other circumstances, a person may need more than one gallon of water per day.

Collecting Water When Supplies Run Low

Most serious preppers do their best to store as much water as they can, but they accept the possibility that regardless of how much water they store, there is a chance that they'll eventually run out. Since you can't survive without water, this means that you'll have to find another source of it if you intend to continue surviving.

One popular system that many preppers have in place is a rainwater harvesting system. These systems can be as simple or as complex as you like. Basically, you just need a catchment to collect rainwater, a simple plumbing system, and a holding tank. In its most simple form, this system is comprised of a roof to collect rainwater, rain gutters for the water to flow through, and rain barrels to store the water.

Many people already have roofs and rain gutters. This means that to construct a rudimentary rainwater harvesting system, they simply need to install some rain barrels at the end of

their gutters. While it's possible to bury these barrels to make them flush with the ground, this can present a problem when it comes to using the water that has been collected. If your rain barrels are buried, you'll need to have some way to get the water out of the barrels. You may need to use a hand pump or a small bucket or ladle of some sort.

A better solution would be to erect elevated stands for the rain barrels to rest on. Then, a valve and hose can be fitted to the bottom of the barrel to make using the water very convenient. If you choose to go this route, make sure you secure the barrels well so that they don't fall over and injure someone or spill all of the precious water you've collected.

Of course, you can't really count on Mother Nature providing rain every time you need to fill your rain barrels. This may mean that you'll need to resort to scavenging for water. In this case, you'll need some way to transport water from the source that you find back to your home or bug out camp. If you have the luxury of transporting

water in your vehicle, you'll simply need some refillable containers. Five-gallon water jugs with screw-on lids would work well for this.

If your home or camp isn't too far away from your water source, you could pull refillable water containers in a heavy-duty garden wagon. You can purchase one of these utility wagons for about $100 at most farm and ranch stores.

They have the ability to transport about 400 pounds at a time. This should be more than adequate for hauling water from your source to your home or camp.

Filtering and Treating Water to Make It Safe to Drink

If you must resort to scavenging for water, you should always treat it so that it is safe to drink. You can purchase commercially available water filters at many camping stores, but these devices aren't 100 percent effective at removing germs, bacteria, and viruses from the water.

 FEMA advises that if you do resort to scavenging for water, you should NOT collect it from a water source that has floating material in it, a bad odor, or a dark color. They also advise you to filter the water prior to treating it to remove as many contaminants as possible.

According to FEMA, boiling is the safest way to purify water for drinking. They advise that water should be boiled at a "rolling boil" for a full minute. Then, let the water cool and oxygenate the water by pouring it back and forth from one container to another. Adding oxygen back into the water using this method should help improve the taste.

The other method of treating water that FEMA rec-ommends is chlorination. To do this properly, they advise to only use regular unscented liquid household bleach that contains 5.25 to 6.0 percent sodium hypochlorite to treat the water. They warn against using bleaches with added cleaners, scented bleaches, or color-safe

 bleaches when chlorinating water for drinking purposes. FEMA also advises people to use bleach from unopened bottles or newly opened bottles because the potency of bleach diminishes over time.

Simply add sixteen drops or one-eighth of a teaspoon to one gallon of untreated water. Stir or shake the container to thoroughly mix the bleach with the water and let this mixture sit for thirty minutes before drinking. FEMA advises that after waiting a full thirty minutes, the water should slightly smell of bleach. If it doesn't, they suggest repeating the procedure and waiting for another fifteen minutes. If after waiting the additional fifteen minutes, the water still doesn't have a slight smell of bleach, they suggest that you discard the water and try collecting it from a different source.

Note: You can and should print this helpful document provided by FEMA and keep it on hand to refer to when you need to remember how to treat water to make it safe for drinking. The link to the document is: www.fema. gov/pdf/library/f&web.pdf.

This document also contains instructions on how to purify water through a process known as distillation. Boiling and chlorination will remove most microorganisms, but according to this FEMA document, distillation will remove the remaining microorganisms as well as remove most impurities that might be in the water.

Distillation can also effectively desalinate salt water and make it safe to drink. Knowing how to distill water is a skill that could come in handy for those of you who live near the coast and have access to water from the ocean.

Warning: You can never be too careful when it comes to purifying water to be used for drinking. Be sure that you precisely follow the steps outlined in the link to the document from FEMA to minimize your chances of becoming sick from drinking water from a dirty source.

Preparing To Help Your Animals Survive Doomsday

It's extremely important to remember that your critters are going to need food and water when doomsday arrives. If you have pets or livestock, don't forget to plan for their daily food and water needs when you are putting up supplies in your prepping cache.

Many preppers keep livestock such as milk goats or milk cows to provide a source of milk while they are in a survival situation. Others keep horses or mules to provide a means of transportation if gas becomes too expensive or unavailable. It's very important to remember that these animals will require much more water per day than a person requires. If you are keeping livestock or if you have pets to care for, be sure to plan accordingly and store plenty of food and water for them, as well.

The worst case scenario would be for your family to have to go without food or water because you didn't prepare and store enough for your animal's needs. Another thing to keep in mind is that you might survive just fine on the items in your food storage, but your horses won't do well eating canned turkey or dehydrated apricots.

When it comes to storing water for livestock, you don't need to be as cautious as you are when you're putting up water for human consumption. Many farm stores sell large water storage tanks that are perfect for storing water for your pets and livestock. They range in sizes from 250 to 1,500 gallons. These tanks aren't cheap, but the fact that your livestock can potentially help you survive doomsday means that they are a prepping expense that is worth paying.

If you simply fill a 1,000-gallon tank and let it sit in the sun for months and months on end, it's likely that an abundant amount of algae will grow inside. When storing

water for livestock, keep in mind that it will stay fresher if you rotate through it occasionally. It will also stay fresher if you keep it out of the direct sunlight. One idea is to cover the tank with an insulated enclosure to shade it and slow it from freezing in the winter.

Keep in mind that if you are going to store large quantities of water for your animals, you'll need some way for the water to get from the tank to their water troughs. This can be accomplished by positioning the tank so that it sits at a higher elevation than the water troughs. Then you can simply attach a hose to the tank, open a valve, and let the water flow with the help of gravity. It can also be accomplished by pumping the water with a hand-powered or pedal-powered pump of some form.

Making Use of the "One Extra" Method When Shopping

Here's a tip that is really useful when it comes to building up a stockpile of food and/or emergency supplies. The tip is to make use of the "one extra" method. If you're buying canned beans and you need one can of beans, buy two and put the second one into storage. If you're buying a package of batteries to use in your flashlight and you only need one, buy two and put the second away for use in emergencies.

Of course it won't be practical to buy two of everything each time you go shopping, especially if you're on a tight budget. Instead, look for items that are on sale  or items that are packaged in special buy one, get one free packages. If you get into the habit of buying one extra whenever you find the right deal, you'll be surprised how quickly your emergency stockpile will build up.

Remember, not many people have the luxury of being able to go out and purchase their entire cache of food storage and emergency supplies all at once. With this in mind, don't let yourself make the mistake of becoming overwhelmed by all the things that need to be purchased.

Keep in mind that Rome wasn't built in a day and your emergency supplies collection won't be either.

This is a good time to bring up a key point that can help keep many preppers from becoming discouraged. If you are building a collection of something like stamps, coins, or baseball cards, you don't go out and buy the entire collection all at once. Instead, you slowly buy items to add to your collection one or two at a time. Over time, the items that you are collecting will grow into an impressively-sized collection.

If you'll keep this in mind when it comes to building a collection of emergency supplies, it will be easier for you to not feel overwhelmed by fixating on all the things that you would eventually like to have in your cache of supplies.

Save Money by Learning the Art of Couponing

Couponing has evolved considerably in recent years. We're no longer talking about simply waiting around until the Sunday paper is delivered to clip a few coupons here and there. The ways that coupons can be collected in this digital day and age are many times greater than they once were.

It's beyond the scope of this book to teach you to be a couponing master; instead, I encourage you to learn to make the most of the couponing experience. With the help of coupons that can be collected and printed from the Internet, it's now possible to find coupons for just about everything you want to buy.

It's not uncommon for master couponers to walk into a store and come out with unbelievable deals such as a shopping cart full of free toilet paper, for example. Having a large stockpile of items like toilet paper could come in pretty handy someday and you can't get a better price than free!

It takes a bit of time and effort to learn how to get the best deals when using coupons, but it's definitely worth putting in the work

to master this skill set. Some of the most prolific preppers are master couponers, and they are amazing at stretching their prepping dollar to get the most from their money.

Stocking Up on Medication and Medical Supplies

Many preppers have medical conditions that require them to be on some form of medication. While you're building your cache of emergency supplies, it's important that you don't forget to stock up on any medications you require.

This can be a bit tricky because many health insurance companies won't let you purchase more than you'll need in the short term. That being said, you might try checking with your pharmacy to see if you can mail order several months' worth of medications in advance. In some cases, you can order three months of medication at a time and receive a discount for filling your prescription in this manner.

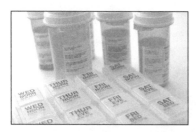 You might also consider speaking with your doctor and telling him or her about your prepping goals. If you express your desire to stock up on supplies to be used in the event of a major emergency, he or she may be able to find ways of helping you, such as giving you free samples of the medications you take to put away for a rainy day.

Remember that, like food, medication is a perishable item, which means it will eventually expire. If you stockpile over-the-counter medications such as aspirin or ibuprofen, you should rotate it out of your cache of supplies before it expires.

Don't forget that in the event of a major emergency, you probably won't be able to walk into your local superstore and buy things like bandages, antiseptic, and other first-aid supplies. It's extremely important to keep in mind that the need for these types of supplies could be quite high depending upon the nature of the doomsday event that you find yourself trying to survive.

Even minor injuries could become life threatening if you don't have the necessary supplies to disinfect and dress wounds. For this reason, emergency medical supplies should be near the top of your list in terms of the level of importance you place on storing them.

Money Saving Tip: You can sometimes buy discounted first-aid supplies at military surplus stores. You might also try contacting local doctors' offices and/or hospitals to

see if they have any supplies that they are throwing out. You might just find that they are willing to give you old medical supplies that they don't have a use for and that they haven't yet used.

Remembering to Take Your Vitamins after Doomsday

As a prepper, your main goal is to stock up on the items that will make it possible for you and your family to survive when things get really bad. This may mean that you might find it a bit difficult to serve up three well-balanced meals to your family every day.

The longer you have to live off your food storage, the less balanced your meals will be in terms of overall nutrition. This will not happen because you didn't prepare well, but because your supplies will start to run low and you'll have fewer choices of food available for you to prepare.

One way to help yourself and your family stay healthy while you're in survival mode is for each of you to take a daily multivitamin. Vitamin supplements are easy to store and they don't take up much space. Better yet, they

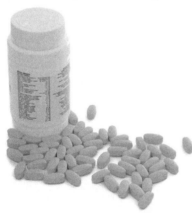

will provide you with essential vitamins and minerals that you might be lacking due to the nature of your diet.

Remember, you may not have the luxury of being able to waltz on into the doctor's office if you happen to get sick. Anything you can do to stay healthy will help you survive until society rebuilds and things get back to some degree of normalcy. Taking daily multivitamins is an easy way to help your body stay healthy, so be sure and store several bottles.

One tip regarding storing vitamins and over-the-counter medications is to look at the expiration dates on the bottles in the store. Find the bottles that are the freshest and buy those. This will increase the length of time that you can keep them stored with your emergency supplies.

Get the Upper Hand by Storing Bartering Items

If you find yourself in the midst of a major doomsday event, you'll likely have a very hard time buying the supplies you're in need of at a store. Stores may not even be open or they may have already been looted by marauders who have completely cleaned out the shelves.

Hopefully you'll have prepared well enough that you'll have the major necessities to survive stored away in your stockpile. The reality is that regardless of how well you prepare, you may find yourself in need of some supplies or services that you just don't have. This is where bartering can come in really handy!

Before the days of supermarkets on every street corner, trading or bartering was a regularly used method of obtaining the things that people needed. During the aftermath of an event like a major natural disaster, this method of commerce will likely become much more common than it is now. The basic principle is that if you have something of value that someone else wants or needs, you can trade it for something that you want or need.

If the doomsday event that you are facing causes extreme hyperinflation, you may not even be able to use cash to get the things you need. We've all heard the stories about how hyperinflation in Germany after World War I created conditions where people couldn't even buy a loaf of bread with a wheelbarrow full of money.

Even though you might not be able to buy the supplies that you need, you may be able to trade for them *if* you have the right kind of items to use for bartering. Let's talk for a minute about what the "right kind" of bartering items might be.

Of course, regular items from your food storage or medical supply cache could be used for bartering, but items that might be more sought after are the luxury items. We're talking about the types of items that aren't necessarily needed to survive, but that many people have become so accustomed to having that they'll do virtually anything to get their hands on them.

Items such as liquor, cigarettes, and chewing tobacco are three examples of items that will be in very high demand.

If you have these types of items stored away to use for bartering for supplies, you'll definitely have the upper hand during the negotiations.

Another type of luxury item that you might not think about storing is simple reading material. If you are stuck in the middle of a doomsday crisis, it's highly likely that the power grid will be down. We live in a world full of people who have become so reliant upon electronic gadgets like televisions, computers, smartphones, iPads, MP3 players, and video games that if the power grid does go down for an extended period of time, people won't know what to do with themselves. Mass boredom will set in and they'll find themselves looking for ways to alleviate this boredom.

When this happens, they'll start searching for reading material to occupy their time and minds with. This is where you come in! If you have taken the time to stock up on books and magazines, you'll have a powerful bargaining chip that you can use to your benefit.

If you don't believe that reading material will be in high demand, think about the last time you found yourself stuck in the waiting room at a doctor's office. How did

you pass the time? If you're like most people, you spent it reading a magazine that you found on a table in the waiting room. In many cases, you probably picked up a magazine that you would have never purchased in the store and started thumbing through it to find something to read. You probably even read some articles that weren't really that interesting to you just to kill time.

Money Saving Tip: Before you head on down to your local book store and start spending your prepping dollars on books and magazines, you should know that you can pick these items up for next to nothing and oftentimes free if you know a couple of simple tricks.

The first trick is to visit your local library and ask them if they have any old magazines or books that they are throwing out. Believe it or not, libraries throw out old books and magazines all the time. When their old books become tattered, they will often throw them out instead of spending the money to have them repaired. Libraries have limited space and magazines are usually distributed monthly. They just don't have the space to store years and years of old magazine issues, so they periodically throw them out or recycle them.

The second trick is to visit doctors' offices and hospitals and ask them to save their old magazines for you. Most of them subscribe to numerous magazines so their patients will have something to read while they are "being patient" and waiting their turn to be seen by a doctor. If you tell them that you'll pick their old magazines up on a monthly basis so that they don't have to hassle with recycling them, you might just get your hands on quite a few free magazines that would be perfect to use when bartering.

The last trick is to visit yard sales. You might not realize it, but the best time to hit a yard sale is on the last day of the sale—just before they are getting ready to put everything away and clean up. If you walk up and say, "I'll give you $5.00 for that box of books that you didn't sell," they'll often say yes. They'll say yes because they're tired of dealing with the yard sale and they don't want to have to pack the books away and continue storing them.

Leverage the Power of Buying in Bulk

When it comes to buying food for your food storage, one of the best ways to get great deals is to buy in bulk. If you shop at wholesale stores such as Costco or Sam's Club, you'll often get much better prices when you buy bulk quantities.

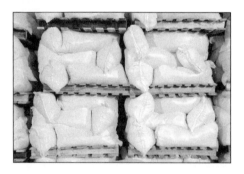

One option for those of you who are on a budget is to get some of your prepper friends together and pool your money for making bulk purchases. Then you can leverage the cost savings that come from buying in bulk without having to come up with all the money yourself.

You might have to repackage some of the items when you divide them, but you'll be able to take advantage of bulk shopping prices without breaking your budget. This is just one of the many creative ways that preppers can band together to help each other prepare for doomsday.

Get Back to Basics and Learn to Preserve Food Now

Another thing that many preppers have in common is that they know how to preserve their own food. This is a skill that today's society is rapidly losing. It's also a skill that is very much worthy of learning while you are preparing for doomsday. We won't teach you how to preserve food in this book. We will, rather, encourage you to develop the skills to be able to use the methods described below.

- **Canning**—When we talk about canning as a way of preserving food, we're not talking about storing food in metal cans. We're talking about storing food in glass jars that have been sterilized and sealed to lock in the freshness. Fruits, vegetables, and even cooked meat can be preserved with this method and safely stored for quite some time.

- **Dehydrating**—This is a method of preserving food that can also be used to preserve fruits, vegetables, or meats. Dehydrated food can be stored and eaten in its dry form or even reconstituted by adding water and cooking it.

- **Smoking**—This is one of the oldest methods of preserving food known to man. Smoking meat is a way of increasing the length of time that it takes for food to spoil. In a post-doomsday world, meat that is obtained via hunting or fishing can be preserved by smoking it. It doesn't last as long as canned meat, but it is an effective method of preserving meat nonetheless.

Now would be a good time to talk about the importance of rotating through your food storage. Don't make the mistake of simply storing a bunch of food and forgetting about it. Food storage isn't like wine in that it gets better as it ages. When you are storing food, make sure that you clearly write the date that you stored the food on each container. Then, organize your food storage in such a way that you'll know where the oldest food is.

As the food begins to near its expiration date, start eating it and replace it with fresh food. The important thing to remember about storing food is that it is a process that never really ends. Since food is perishable, you'll want to rotate it into your daily meals as it approaches its expiration date. Then, as you replace the food you have eaten, you'll always have a fresh supply of food in your food storage.

This brings up another important point. You should consider storing the types of food that your family will actually eat. This way, you can easily rotate it into your daily meals and your family won't feel like they are eating food storage.

Money Saving Tip: If you'll learn to preserve your own food with these methods, you'll find that you can buy raw fruits, vegetables, and meats in bulk and preserve them yourself much cheaper than you can purchase commercially canned food products.

Many preppers grow vegetable gardens for the sole purpose of being able to can or dehydrate their crops for storing in their food storage. Even if you don't grow your own garden, you can save money by attending your local farmers' market and making deals with farmers to buy vegetables in bulk from them.

 If you're friendly with your neighbors who happen to grow gardens, they may even share their harvest with you in exchange for some of the jams or jellies that you prepare. People love homemade jam and if they think you'll share with them, they'll often be more than happy to share their extra fruits with you.

Learn How to Obtain Food in a Post-Doomsday World

Regardless of how well you prepare, you may find yourself in a situation where you need to acquire more food. We are of course assuming that society has broken down to the point that you can't simply waltz into your local grocery store and purchase the food that you want or need.

One option is to dip into your stash of barter items and trade some items or services that you can offer for food that you need. Another option for those who live in a rural area is to hunt, fish, or gather food. If you do, in fact, live in a rural area, there is a good chance that you already know how to hunt and fish. Hunting and fishing are favorite pastimes for country folks all over the world, but if you aren't from the country, you may not have this skill set yet.

It's natural to think that all you need to do is own a gun and fishing pole and if you ever need to use these items to gather food, you'll be able to. The truth of the matter is that to be successful at hunting and fishing, you'll need to have some degree of expertise.

Let's take a look at hunting for a minute first. To be a successful hunter, you need to first understand your quarry. For example, if you plan on hunting deer, you need to understand the type of habitat where they are most likely to be found. You need to understand their feeding patterns, as well. The more you know about your quarry, the better the chances are that you'll actually be able to put some meat on the table.

You also need to be proficient with your weapon of choice. Whether it's a gun, a bow and arrow, or even snares, you need to be quite skilled with them to be successful. The higher degree of skill that you have with them, the better your chances of being successful will be.

If you are fortunate enough to harvest an animal for food, you'll need to know what to do with it so that you can actually eat the meat. Field dressing a deer isn't something that you want to learn from a book during a time when you are feeling the pressure to provide some food for your family. Then there's the matter of preserving the meat so that you can make it last. It would be quite wasteful to harvest a deer and only get one or two meals from it before it spoiled.

Are you starting to get the picture here? While it's definitely true that meat can be obtained via hunting, fishing, or trapping, it's highly advisable to develop the skills to be successful before you actually need to rely on them.

The same holds true when it comes to gathering edible plants in the forest. The forest can provide a bounty of edible plants and berries, but gathering these types of foods can be deadly if your skill level isn't up to snuff. What you think might be an edible berry could be quite poisonous. Eat the wrong berries or mushrooms and you could become ill or even die.

There are plenty of field guide books that can help you properly identify edible plants and berries and you should have a few of them stored away with your emergency supplies. Keep in mind that you won't have the luxury of hopping onto the Internet to look for a picture to help you identify which plants and berries are actually edible while you're trying to survive doomsday. For this reason, it would be wise to have a large collection of field guides and manuals on hand to refer to should the need ever arise.

Better yet, since we are talking about "prepping" here, it would be wiser of you to get some training from someone who is experienced at gathering edible plants and berries. Books are great, but they're no substitute for experience! If you have taken the time to hone your gathering skills, when and if the time comes that you need to put these skills into use, you'll be much better off. You can always refer to your field guides when you need them, but the fact that you thought ahead and actually got some training on how to properly identify which plants you should and should not be eating will really pay off in the long run.

Turn Your Survival Food into Meals That Satisfy

One can only live on dehydrated food for so long, and when it comes to living off of your food storage there is a good chance that you'll quickly grow tired of eating cornbread for every meal. Part of preparing to survive doomsday is knowing how to prepare meals with the food that you actually have in your food storage. Your family won't appreciate it much if the only thing you can do with your hundreds of pounds of stored wheat is make tortillas.

Speaking of food storage, be sure that you store items that you will actually use. Along with the items that you are storing away in your food storage, you should keep recipes that you can use to prepare meals with the particular items that you have on hand.

Additionally, be sure to stock up on the little things that can transform your meals from merely being food that you can survive on to enjoyable and satisfying meals. Oftentimes having an assortment of spices on hand can take a very bland and boring meal and transform it into a tasty feast.

Keep in mind that spices are cheap and easy to store. They don't take up much space and they have a very long shelf life. Do yourself and your family a favor and the next time you're at the grocery store, buy some extra bottles of spices and put them away with your food storage items.

Money Saving Tip: You can usually find really big bottles of spices at wholesale stores like Costco. Pound for pound, the cost is much lower when you buy them this way. If you have friends who are into prepping, you can go in together and buy large quantities of spices. Then you can divide them and repackage them. This way, you'll get much more for your money and you'll be helping your fellow preppers meet their prepping goals at the same time.

Becoming Prepared To Defend Yourself and Your Property

In the world that we live in today, most people give very little thought to preparing to defend themselves, their families, or their properties. We live in a world where you can just grab your cell phone and call 911 whenever you feel threatened. In most cases, within minutes of calling for help, the police will arrive and come to your rescue.

During a major emergency that leads to the breakdown of civilized society, this won't likely be the case. If you don't believe this, take a minute and remember back to what became of New Orleans after hurricane Katrina caused all of the devastating flooding.

In some cases, the police themselves fled the city because of the widespread rioting and marauding that was going on. The police were drastically outnumbered and there were even reports of actual police officers being shot at! Now, imagine this kind of chaos multiplied across hundreds of cities. Instead of this insanity being isolated to one city like New Orleans, cities all across the country and maybe even all across the world would be in the same state of disarray.

Most serious preppers believe that the responsibility of protecting themselves, their families, and their possessions will lie solely on their own shoulders. Consequently, they take the matter of preparing to defend what is theirs very seriously.

Let's take a look at the matter of self-defense for a minute. Most preppers break this down into two categories.

Firearms

The first category is the use of weapons to defend yourself and your property. This can include many types of weapons, but in most cases preppers tend to focus on stocking up on firearms and ammunition.

While some preppers don't see a place for firearms in their prepping plans, this is usually the exception rather than the rule. Most people who are seriously into prepping would consider their guns to be one of the most important elements of their plan to survive doomsday.

Guns can provide many benefits for preppers. In the hands of a skilled outdoorsman, they can help to put food on the table. They can protect life, virtue, and property from those who would threaten to take it. They can also provide a sense of comfort during times of turmoil.

If law and order breaks down and the streets are filled with people who intend to do you harm or take what is yours, having access to a supply of firearms will be very comforting for you and your family. Just knowing that your family is well-armed will provide a sense of security and comfort that will be hard to beat after a doomsday event takes place.

A fourth benefit to being well-armed is that there is a certain psychological deterrent that guns tend to carry.

If people know that you're well-armed and prepared to defend yourself and your property, they will be less likely to mess with you. Think about it: People tend to prey on the individuals that they perceive to be weak. If you're armed and prepared to defend what is yours, you won't appear weak and marauders will want to pick an easier target.

We won't get into the brands of firearms you should stock up on because this is a hotly debated subject. That being said, let's have a brief discussion about the caliber of firearms that many preppers prefer. It has often been said that the best kind of gun is the one that you actually have with you. This basically means that having any gun is better than not having one at all.

This is true to a certain extent, but most preppers prefer to stock up on guns and ammunition that they think will be of the most use to them when things get really ugly. More specifically, they prefer guns that are chambered in commonly available military calibers.

The most commonly available military rounds are 7.62 x 39mm, which is the caliber of the extremely popular AK-47 as well as the widely used SKS. Another caliber of preference is 5.56 x 45mm, which is the caliber that the M16 and AR-15 both shoot. The other commonly

 preferred caliber is 9mm, which is the most commonly used handgun ammunition for military and police use.

The primary reason that these are the most popular calibers is because of their widespread availability all around the world. The fact that these calibers are so commonly used means that the price to buy ammunition in bulk is much lower than with popular sporting gun calibers.

Keep in mind that a gun without ammunition is nothing more than a fancy club. It's impossible to predict how long civil unrest will carry on when doomsday comes knocking on your door. If you own firearms that are chambered in these commonly available military calibers, you can buy the ammunition in bulk and keep thousands of rounds on hand for a fraction of the price of buying popular sporting ammunition. Most preppers agree that when it comes to ammunition, more is always better, so being able to buy ammo in bulk at a discounted rate is a big advantage for budget-conscious preppers.

Another advantage of sticking to the most common military type of firearms is that guns like the AK-47 are known worldwide for their ease of use and reliability. They are designed and battle proven to function in the worst of conditions. Should they ever break and you find yourself in search of parts to repair them, your chances of being able to barter for popular replacement parts are much higher than if you simply owned sporting rifles.

Yet another advantage of staying with guns that are chambered in commonly available military calibers is that, because the ammunition is cheaper to purchase, it's also cheaper to shoot. If it's cheaper to shoot it's possible to spend more time training with the gun. There's no substitute for training when it comes to firearms. The more time you spend training with a particular gun, the more proficient you'll be with it. The more proficient you are with your gun, the higher your odds of surviving should you ever need to use it to defend yourself.

Money Saving Tip: If you order your ammunition online, you can often get some really great deals. One good place

to buy inexpensive ammunition in bulk is a website called www.cheaperthandirt. com. This website sells military calibers of ammo in bulk at much better prices than you can get at your local sporting goods store.

Hand-to-Hand Combat

The second category preppers should be concerned about when it comes to self-defense preparation is close contact hand-to-hand combat. Getting the proper training in some kind of hand-to-hand style of fighting can mean the difference between life and death in certain circumstances.

When it comes to up close and personal self-defense training, this is a skill that takes years to master. Don't think for a minute that you can attend a weekend seminar and you'll magically have all the training you need to defend yourself in a real world struggle. No matter how good the instructors were or how comprehensive the seminar was, it takes a lot of time and practice to be able to develop the skills well enough so that when you actually need to rely on them, they won't let you down.

Many preppers spend years practicing hand-to-hand combat. They repeat the same drills and exercises hundreds, if not thousands, of times. They do this so that when they are placed in a dangerous situation, the moves will be second nature to them and they can act

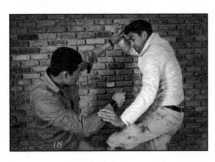

without thinking and successfully fend off their attacker.

While it's true that it takes a lot of work to master hand-to-hand combat training, it's important that you not let this overwhelm you to the point that you don't get started right away. Remember, as with anything that has to do with prepping, you have to start somewhere and the best place to start is at the beginning.

The fact that this takes so long to master can actually work out in your favor. Self-defense training can be physically taxing and a fringe benefit of routinely training your body in this way is that your level of physical fitness will improve dramatically. This brings us to our next chapter, which is on preparing your body to survive a doomsday event.

Preparing Your Body to Survive Doomsday

When doomsday finally does arrive, many of the tasks that we used to be able to rely on technology for will have to be done by hand. This may even include getting from point A to point B. If the transportation system goes down, you may find that you can't just hop in your car when you need to go somewhere. Gas may not be available or it may be so expensive that you can't afford to purchase it.

Many preppers have several evacuation or "bug out" plans in place. Bugging out means that things have gotten so bad at your home or in the city that you live in that you're forced to leave for your own safety. Many bug out plans call for grabbing your bug out bag and evacuating on foot. (For more about bugging out, turn to Section 2.) You may have to travel quite a few miles on foot, and if you're not physically fit, you might not be able to make it to your bug out location at all.

In preparation for such a time, most serious preppers feel that becoming physically fit is very important. The fitter you are, the better prepared you'll be to cope with the manual labor that you'll be forced to endure while surviving doomsday.

Fortunately, getting fit is something that can be done without spending a lot of money. Of course, you can get a gym membership, but you can also get fit by hitting the streets and starting a walking or running regimen.

Going to the gym will undoubtedly offer more options in terms of the types of exercise equipment you'll have access to, but there are plenty of exercises such as push-ups, sit-ups, and pull-ups that can be done without spending a dime. With a little creativity, you can become quite fit without ever stepping foot in the gym.

The bottom line is that the better shape you're in physically before doomsday hits us, the easier surviving will be for you. You'll be kicking yourself if one day you end up having to try to survive while you're still overweight and out of shape. The best advice that anyone can give you regarding this matter is to start getting in shape *now*.

Planning for Your Post-Doomsday Transportation Needs

There are many different scenarios that could lead to the breakdown of society. Many preppers predict that whether it's extreme hyperinflation or a massive solar flare, our transportation system will be down and unusable. If this happens, you may not be able to hop in the family car to reach your destination.

Of course, one option is to travel on foot, and if you took the last chapter to heart, you will have taken the time to get yourself physically fit before doomsday arrives. Traveling on foot is one option, but you won't be able to cover much ground if you find yourself hoofing it. This is, of course, a very slow way of traveling.

Perhaps a better option would be to make sure that you have some good bicycles on hand. If you're pedaling a bicycle, you'll be able to travel many more miles than if you are limited to traveling on foot.

Money Saving Tip: Craigslist is a great place to find used bicycles at very reasonable prices. Do yourself a big favor and avoid the allure of the shiny bikes with low price tags that are typically found in big-box department stores. For the same amount of money, you can usually find a previously used, yet much higher quality bike. If you spend much time riding a bike, you'll soon realize that there is quite a big difference in the ride-ability and durability between the inexpensive bikes found in super shopping centers and quality name brand secondhand bikes.

If you live in a rural area, you may want to consider getting some horses if there is money in the budget. When it comes time to survive the hard times that are ahead of us, horses can provide a great mode of transportation. They can also be used to perform work. A horse or mule can be trained to carry a rider, transport supplies when wearing a pack saddle, or even pull farm equipment or wagons.

Due to the tough financial times that many Americans have been experiencing in recent years, the prices of good horses have decreased substantially. This means that as a buyer, you have plenty of leverage. Don't settle for just any old broken-down horse. Be sure and buy one that has been suitably trained for the purpose you have in mind. The horse market is so soft right now that you can

find well-trained horses for very affordable prices.

Should you find yourself having to get around on foot during the winter months, having snowshoes on hand can really make a big difference. If you live in a part of the country that gets a lot of snow, there is a possibility that the snow-plows won't be clearing the roads for you after a major disaster causes a doomsday event. This means that you might find yourself having to trudge through the snow on foot. If you've ever tried walking for some distance through deep snow without snowshoes, you know how tremendously taxing it can be on your body.

Remember, you can't pick and choose the time of year that a natural or economic disaster could lead to a doomsday event. There's just as good a chance of it happening in the dead of winter as there is of it happening during the nice summer months.

Heating Your Home without Electricity or Gas

You should plan on the electricity grid going down after a major emergency. You should also plan on the natural gas supply lines being down. This means that if your home is heated with either of these utilities, you may not have a way of keeping your family warm.

This next bit of advice is one that doesn't come cheaply, but could save your life if you are forced to try and survive during the dead of winter. The advice is to equip your home with a wood-burning stove. Exactly how much this will set you back will depend on the model of stove that you purchase as well as whether you have the time and skills to install it yourself.

If you do have the time and skills to do the installation yourself, an entry-level woodstove can be installed for about $2,000. If you don't have the necessary skills, it will cost you significantly to pay someone to install it. Many people don't realize the importance of having a woodstove until it dawns on them that they can't heat their home because the power or gas has been turned off for one reason or another.

Along with installing a good woodstove in your home comes the responsibility of stocking up on firewood. If you live in a rural area, you have the option of cutting your own firewood, which will reduce the cost considerably. If you aren't able to cut your own firewood, you'll have no other option than to purchase it.

Firewood can be purchased in "rounds," meaning that each piece is cut to length but not split. It's usually a bit cheaper to purchase it this way because your supplier doesn't have to go to the trouble or incur the cost of splitting it themselves. While it is a bit cheaper to purchase firewood this way, you'll have to split it before you can burn it. If you're fit enough to do this yourself, it can

be great exercise. If not, you'll need to purchase firewood that is already split.

A good tip is to arrange to see the wood you are interested in purchasing before you have it delivered. Check to make sure that the wood you are thinking about buying has been seasoned and stored properly. This means that it has had plenty to time to dry out. If you buy green wood that hasn't been adequately seasoned, it will burn very poorly and you'll be really frustrated with it.

Some firewood suppliers cut corners (no pun intended) and the wood will be split but it won't be split into small enough pieces to actually use. If you order a shipment of wood before looking at it, you may find out that you'll have to do more splitting to make the pieces of wood small enough to burn well in your stove.

Making Sure That You Have a Way to Cook Your Food

Much of the food that you put up in your food storage will already be cooked and preserved, but you and your family will enjoy eating it much more if you have a way of heating it up. If you've stored wheat or corn for grinding into flour or cornmeal, you'll need a source of heat to make bread or cornbread.

One option is to cook on or in your woodstove. If you thought ahead, you would have purchased a woodstove that has a cooktop. This will mean that your wood-burning stove will be able to act as both a heat source and a cooking appliance. To be able to cook inside your woodstove, you can make use of cast-iron Dutch ovens. These heavy cast-iron pots are designed for cooking when they are placed in the coals of a fire. You can cook everything in a Dutch oven from stew to bread, which is one of the reasons they are such versatile and useful items for preppers to have on hand.

If you find yourself without electricity or gas during the hot summer months, you aren't going to want to fire up your woodstove just to cook a can of beans. Sure, you'd be able to warm your food up, but your house would become so hot that you'd be absolutely miserable.

A better solution would be to cook your food in a BBQ grill. You can pick up used BBQ grills for very little at yard sales during the summer. You can use either a propane grill or one that is designed to burn charcoal. A propane grill is fine if you have plenty of propane stored away, but propane can be quite expensive and depending on how

long you're without power or gas, you may run out of the supply of propane that you have stored.

Perhaps a better solution would be to use a BBQ grill that is designed to burn charcoal. You don't have to burn commercially manufactured charcoal briquettes in these grills. Instead, you can burn the same wood that you have stockpiled for your woodstove. This is an ideal solution for cooking when the utility grid goes down because it's a cheap and easy way to warm your food or even bake bread if you use a Dutch oven.

Another alternative is to use a solar oven. There are plenty of free plans on the Internet that will show you how to construct a homemade solar oven. You can also purchase commercially made solar ovens that are lightweight and easily transportable. These ovens are a bit more limited than cooking in a BBQ grill with charcoal or wood, but they are still quite useful. One advantage that they have over a BBQ grill is that they don't require any fuel. All you need is the heat from the sun and you're in business. However, if the sun isn't shining, you won't be able to cook anything in them at all.

Know How to Make Fire Before You Need It

You may be one of those people who are going all in and you might stock up on a pallet full of matches. Regardless of how many matches you have, if you haven't developed the skills necessary to properly start a fire, you're going to find yourself quite frustrated.

Starting a fire doesn't have to be difficult, but if you don't know some basic things about this, you might as well not have any matches at all. You should take the time to practice this skill in an approved fire pit well before you need to build your first post-doomsday fire.

If you keep these simple tips in mind, you'll be fine when it comes to starting a fire. Regardless of whether you are working with matches or flint and steel, you need three basic elements to start a fire. These elements are heat, fuel, and oxygen.

Your heat source can be anything from matches to a fire bow. Even if you're using a brand new butane lighter, the most important thing you'll need to get a fire started is called "tinder." Tinder is very fine dry combustible material. This can be anything from paper to dry fluffy cattail duff. The important thing to remember is that your tinder has to easily catch a flame and it has to be very dry to do that.

It's this tinder bundle that is going to catch the initial flame. You'll then feed the burning tinder bundle to make the flame grow into a self-sustaining fire. When you have a burning bundle of tinder, slowly feed it pieces of wood that are progressively larger and larger. The main thing to know about this stage of the game is that you'll need to carefully feed the fire bigger pieces of kindling until enough heat has built up in the fire to sustain the combustion of large pieces of firewood.

Once you have enough heat built up in the fire, you can feed it full-sized pieces of firewood and it will continue burning on its own. This may sound very straightforward and easy, but you wouldn't believe how difficult it can be when you're cold and stressed. It really does take skill and practice to be able to start a fire quickly and, more importantly, keep the fire going.

This is one of those things that preppers can do now that won't cost very much money at all. Even if you don't live in a rural part of the country where you can practice making fire anywhere you like, you shouldn't have too much trouble finding a campground or a park that has approved fire pits for you to practice in.

Storing Fuel for Use after Doomsday

During a doomsday crisis, you probably won't be able to roll on into your favorite gas station and fill up your car. This means that you'll want to store any fuel you'll need ahead of time or you'll have to scavenge for it.

Storing fuel—whether it is gasoline, diesel, or propane—comes with unique challenges. Gasoline is perhaps the  most difficult to store because it is so combustible. Many municipalities have ordinances in place that restrict exactly how many gallons of fuel you are legally allowed to keep on hand. They do this for safety reasons, as most people don't have the proper facilities to be able to safely store large quantities of gasoline or diesel fuel.

Whether you are storing gas or diesel, the important thing to keep in mind is that it does have a shelf life. Like other perishable items, the shelf life of fuel can be prolonged if it is properly stored. Ideally, fuel should be stored in a cool, dark, and well-ventilated area (never indoors). Before storing any gasoline or diesel fuel, a fuel-stabilizer such as STA-BIL should be added to it. This preservative is designed to prolong the shelf life of the fresh fuel you are storing for up to a year or more.

Propane is perhaps the easiest of fuels to store, as you can safely keep it in very large propane tanks. Depending upon where you live, you may be able to rent a 300- to 500-gallon propane tank from your local propane

distributor. Propane has a much longer shelf life than gasoline or diesel, but it's still advisable to consult with your propane supplier to find out how long they recommend storing it.

Warning: Consult with your local authorities about how much fuel you are legally allowed to store and how it should be stored in your area.

The Importance of Having the Right Tools on Hand

When that dreaded doomsday eventually does come around, having a good supply of tools on hand will be very important. Some of the most basic tools to keep on hand are hammers, axes, hatchets, and shovels. With these simple hand tools, you can do everything from burying solid waste and garbage to building a shelter.

The last thing you want to be doing during an emergency is trying to fashion makeshift tools out of items that you happen to scavenge. You may find yourself with no other option than to fashion makeshift tools, but without some basic hand tools, doing that may be very difficult.

In addition to the tools already mentioned, you should have a set of mechanic's tools that includes wrenches, sockets and ratchets, pliers, screwdrivers, and more. You never know when you'll have to repair something that you need to survive. Having the tools on hand that will enable you to perform repairs will make surviving much easier.

Even if you aren't a skilled mechanic, you'll need to have tools on hand. With a little ingenuity, you'll be able to figure out how to do some basic repairs. If you don't have the tools on hand, however, you'll be out of luck.

You may find that you can track down someone who is mechanically inclined enough to do the necessary repairs for you. It's likely that you'll be able to barter their mechanical skills for something that you have that is of value to them, but without the right tools, they won't be able to help you even if they wanted to.

Perhaps some of the most important tools that you should have on hand are good-quality knives. Survival experts love to debate about what the ultimate survival knife actually is. The reason they spend so much time arguing over this issue is that there isn't one particular best

knife. Some knives excel at performing delicate tasks like skinning game, while others excel at tasks like chopping and hacking. Instead of trying to settle on just one knife that will work well in every scenario, you should have several in your collection. Then, you'll be able to choose the best tool for the job at hand instead of trying to make one tool work for every job.

Storing good-quality knives is important, but regardless of how well a particular knife has been made, it won't stay sharp forever. You should plan on your knives becoming dull as you use them and include a good-quality knife sharpening kit with your emergency supplies. Here's another skill that you should develop before you need to rely on it. No matter how fancy the knife sharpening kit you buy is, it takes a skilled hand to sharpen a knife properly. Spend the time now to learn how to do this right ahead of time. It's a skill that won't cost you anything to learn and you'll be glad that you did when you have the ability to put a razor's edge back on your trusty old skinning knife.

While we're on the subject of tools that would be handy to have on hand, let's not forget the ever popular multi-tool. Leatherman, Gerber, and many others make very good multitools. These tools are like having a tool box in your pocket! They can be used for so many tasks that everyone should have one. Once you buy one and start using it, you'll wonder how you ever lived without it.

 When it comes to purchasing multitools, it's worth the money to splurge on the name brand models. Don't make the mistake of buying one of the really cheap knockoffs and thinking that it will perform on par with a good-quality name brand multitool. These knockoffs might look similar in appearance, but most of them really are just pieces of junk. They aren't built nearly as well and oftentimes

they'll break when you are really counting on them to work.

***Money Saving Tip*:** Yard and garage sales are great places to find used tools for sale. It's better to buy good-quality used tools than low-quality new tools. Many of the popular wholesale tool stores carry low-quality tools at very attractive prices. Those unbelievably low prices can quickly turn into nightmares when you realize the tools are so low in quality that they aren't able to perform their intended jobs.

Another great place to find quality used tools is Craigslist. Due to the tough economic times that many Americans are currently facing, many mechanics have been forced to sell off their good tools for pennies on the dollar just to make ends meet. For this very same reason, pawn shops are often good places to find great prices on high-quality used tools.

Communication Devices That Will Work after Doomsday

History has proven that when natural disasters hit, the communication grid is often one of the first things to go down. Most preppers plan on the land lines and cellular phone networks being down for an extended period of time after doomsday comes calling.

While traditional communication services will likely be of no use to us, there are still some basic things you can do to maintain some ability to communicate with your immediate family, friends, and the outside world.

One of the simplest types of communication devices that will still work after doomsday are two-way radios or walkie-talkies. The two most popular types are FRS (Family Radio Service) or GMRS (General Mobile Radio Service). These little two-way radios are inexpensive and can be purchased at most major sporting goods stores as well as many superstores.

These walkie-talkies will provide line of sight communications and are typically limited to within a few miles of effective range. They transmit at low power levels, but they can still be very useful short-distance communication devices during emergencies.

Another option is to purchase HAM radios. A HAM radio requires a license to operate, but the advantage they have over FRS-type radios is that they can broadcast at much higher power levels. Many preppers migrate toward the HAM radio option for its increased power and versatility. With a good HAM radio, you can broadcast and receive messages on a wide variety of frequencies, which makes them the most versatile type of communication radios to have on hand.

While we're on the subject of communication devices, we should talk briefly about emergency radios. Having a good emergency radio on hand means that you'll be able to receive important broadcasts and news from your local authorities. There are several types of emergency radios to choose from, but one very important feature that you should look for is a hand crank. If you purchase an emergency radio that has a hand crank, you'll be able to charge it up at any time and position yourself to receive any important news that the authorities happen to be broadcasting.

Another very handy device to have on hand would be a portable programmable scanner. With a scanner, you can preprogram your local emergency frequencies into it, which could help you keep up to date about what is going on in the area where you are trying to survive.

Keep in mind that you'll need a way to power these devices since the electrical grid will likely be down. Make sure that if you'll be including these devices in your prepping plans you have some way to charge the batteries.

Preparing to Have Electricity after Doomsday

One thing most preppers agree on is that there is a very high likelihood that when doomsday hits, the electrical grid will go down for some period of time. This means that if you intend to have any form of electricity, you'll need to be prepared to generate it yourself.

Don't let the idea of generating your own electricity scare you. There are a few very easy-to-use options when it comes to generating electricity on a small scale. Perhaps the most popular is to purchase portable solar panels with integrated rechargeable battery packs that can be used to charge small battery-powered electronic devices.

Some designers have begun to integrate solar panels into backpacks for charging portable electronic devices. One important thing to keep in mind is that it's easier to conserve electricity than it is to generate it. This means that the electronic devices you plan to stock up on should be very efficient. For example, if you plan to store flashlights, be sure that they use the super-efficient LED bulb technology and that they run on rechargeable batteries that you can charge with your portable solar-charging system.

Another option is to keep a portable gas- or diesel-powered generator on hand. Honda makes some small portable generators that are very fuel efficient. For example, their EU2000i model will run for about ten hours on a mere one gallon of gasoline. When gas will be in short supply, having a portable generator that is fuel efficient will really pay off.

As long as we're talking about having electricity after doomsday, it's important to bring up the possibility of an EMP (electromagnetic pulse) being the cause of doomsday. Many preppers believe that a massive solar flare from our sun is due to hit the Earth soon. They also believe that this solar flare will cause an intense EMP to strike the Earth. Scientists predict that if the EMP pulse is strong enough, it could destroy the electrical circuitry of most, if not all, unprotected electronic devices.

What then is a "protected device"? Well, for the sensitive circuitry in electronic devices to be protected from the effects of an EMP, the circuitry must be adequately shielded. This can be accomplished by storing the devices in a specially insulated box called a "Faraday cage."

This is simply a box or enclosure constructed of a conductive material and insulation. The theory is that since the contents are insulated from the conductive material that forms the outside of the box, they will be protected from any EMP pulses. This sounds quite technical, but it's really not. As a matter of fact, there are plenty of free plans available on the Internet that show you exactly how to construct a homemade Faraday cage with materials that are commonly available at your local hardware store.

The three main takeaways from this chapter are: First, make sure that you prepare for a way to charge batteries with some form of alternative energy source. Second, make sure the electronic devices that you plan to use are energy efficient and that you have rechargeable batteries and chargers for them stored away. Third, make sure that you store these devices in a Faraday cage to ensure that if a solar flare or a nuclear e-bomb were to cause a massive EMP, you will still be able to use your devices afterwards.

Keeping the Lights On When the Power Goes Out

Let's face it. If you find yourself trying to survive after doomsday, it's going to be a scary time. Your world will be turned upside down and anything that can provide comfort will be very important. Believe it or not, something as simple as having light during the night can be very comforting. Of course, you'll need light just to perform simple tasks after the sun goes down, but just having something to take the edge off the darkness will do wonders for your morale.

One option is to go old school and use oil lamps. Oil lamps were used for hundreds of years as a source of light before the electric light bulb replaced them. One advantage of oil lamps is that they'll burn for quite some time without using much oil. The problem with oil lamps, however, is that they can pose a fire risk if they are bumped and knocked over. They also aren't ideal for carrying around to provide light in different locations. Simply put, they do provide light but they're not really a good replacement for a flashlight. Despite their limitations, it's probably a good idea to have a few of these old-fashioned lamps packed away with your emergency supplies.

Another option is to purchase hand crank flashlights. These flashlights have a crank that you turn for a couple of minutes and when you've finished cranking, an internal battery will be charged enough to provide light for a few minutes. They usually come equipped with LED bulb technology, which makes them bright enough to use. However, since the LEDs don't use much electricity, they remain lit for quite some time between cranking cycles.

The advantage that these flashlights have over oil lamps is that you can easily take them from job to job without ever having to worry about spilling the oil or starting a fire. They can also produce a directional beam of light so that you can aim the light exactly where you need it. With some models, you can adjust the beam and they'll double as a small battery-powered lantern.

 A third option is to stock up on solar-powered lights. The price of this technology has come way down in recent years and the quality of these devices has improved quite a bit as well. You can purchase a solar lighting fixture that has a small solar panel tethered to the fixture by a long cord. This would make it possible to mount the solar panel outside in the direct sunlight and then to mount the lighting fixture inside to provide interior light exactly where you need it. It's true that these solar lights are designed for outdoor use, but when you're in survival mode, with a little bit of creativity, you can make use of them indoors quite easily.

Dealing with the Dirty Job of Waste Disposal

As a general rule, we don't give much thought to disposing of our garbage or our sewage in the modern world we live in. We simply haul our trash to the curb and when we wake up the next day, it has magically disappeared. When we use the toilet, we simply flush and never give another thought as to where the smelly stuff actually goes. All we care about is that it does, in fact, go away. When something eventually does go wrong with this process, it's a very big deal and we run frantically looking for the nearest plunger to prevent a messy spill.

Well, what if you hauled your garbage to the curb and no one came to pick it up? What if you flushed the toilet and nothing happened? Both of these scenarios are very real possibilities if a doomsday event were to take place. If civilization were to break down for one reason or another, the chances of your garbage man diligently showing up on Tuesday morning to haul your trash off would be very slim. You need water to flush your toilet, and if the city water lines that supply your home with fresh water are cut off, you won't want to use what precious water you have on hand for flushing the toilet.

This presents the question: How will you dispose of your solid waste products after doomsday? Well, many preppers plan to dig holes far away from their living quarters and bury it in the ground. The idea of burying paper and cardboard doesn't tend to make people feel squeamish, but the idea of burying human waste sure does.

The important thing to keep in mind is that in order to maintain a healthy living environment that is as free from disease as possible, it's important to maintain sanitation. Garbage that consists of paper products can be burned, but human waste is a different matter altogether.

In a doomsday scenario that lasts for a prolonged period of time, you're going to want to limit your family's exposure to human waste as much as you possibly can. This may mean using a portable latrine that consists of a plastic bag to catch the waste and then burying the bags. It could also mean constructing an outhouse with a deep hole to catch the waste. Regardless of which method of sanitation you choose, you should do all you can to keep the waste as far away from where you live, eat, and sleep as possible.

With sanitation in mind, it's a good idea to stock up on plenty of plastic garbage bags. There are so many uses for these items that the more you have on hand, the better.

Money Saving Tip: Why not make the most of a recycling opportunity while you are prepping for doomsday? Every time you go to the store to shop for groceries, you probably bring home several plastic bags. If you're responsible with them, you probably already take them to the recycler . . . but maybe you shouldn't. These bags are free, so why not save them for use after doomsday arrives?

Ask your friends to save their empty plastic shopping bags for you and in no time at all, you'll have more bags than you know what to do with. They're easy to store since they can be tightly compacted, so you could stash hundreds, if not thousands, of these bags away with your prepping supplies and they won't cost you a dime!

Don't Underestimate the Importance of Cleanliness

Surviving doomsday will mean that you will have to sacrifice many of your modern conveniences. If you're accustomed to taking two showers a day, you're going to have to give this luxury up. Water will quickly become a precious commodity, which may make it difficult to maintain the same level of cleanliness that you are used to.

Of course, you're going to want to stock up on soap and other personal hygiene supplies, but you'll have to be resourceful about how you choose to use them. Maintaining cleanliness will be very important when it comes to keeping survivors healthy.

Keeping in mind that you'll likely be rationing water, you can and should stock up on a large supply of antibacterial liquid hand sanitizer. This product can be used to keep your hands free from germs without you needing to dip into your precious water supply.

Money Saving Tip: When it comes to using hand and bath towels, you don't want to have to use precious water to wash them every time you use them. A better solution might be to stock up on industrial-sized rolls of paper hand towels. These rolls can be purchased in bulk at stores like Costco and they only cost about $35 for a (7-count) case of 800-foot rolls. That's about $5 a roll, which works out to less than a penny a foot! Now that's cheap!

Don't Forget to Stock Your Bug Out Survival Caches

Depending on the nature of the event that brings doomsday upon us, you may find that bugging in and trying to survive at home just won't work. This may be especially true if you live in a metropolitan area, where marauders are trying to steal people's supplies.

Major natural disasters tend to bring on riots, and riots tend to bring out the worst in people. These people will be amped up with panic and rage and they'll often do things that they normally wouldn't do. People get caught up in the chaos of a riot and, like sheep, they'll do what others are doing just for the sake of following the crowd.

Likewise, you shouldn't underestimate the great lengths that people will go to when they are put into a situation where they are forced to watch their children go hungry. Faced with this scenario, people who would normally be placid, law-abiding citizens will do virtually anything to secure food and supplies. This includes resorting to violent measures so that they can take the supplies that you have so diligently stocked up on.

If the danger to your family becomes too intense, you'll probably have to bug out and leave your home. Hopefully you will have taken the advice about having a good evacuation plan to heart and you'll be prepared to bug out and get your family to a safer location.

If you do find yourself having to bug out, your chances of surviving will be much greater if you have several small bug out caches hidden in strategic locations. These caches can be hidden virtually anywhere. You can store these supplies in places ranging from storage units to underground waterproof containers. The possibilities are only limited by your imagination.

There are two types of bug out caches that you should consider having. The first is a small hidden supply of emergency supplies that you can get to on foot or by car on the way to your planned bug out location. Think of these caches like little minimarts that you can rely on to restock the supplies you'll need while traveling to a more permanent and safe bug out location. These caches might contain items like food, water, weapons, tools, fuel, first-aid supplies, and clothing.

It's a good idea to have these caches hidden along all possible evacuation routes that you have in your bug out plan. Then, no matter which route you end up taking, you know that there is a safe spot for you to stop and restock your supplies.

The other type of bug out cache consists of the supplies you will have stored at a more permanent bug out location. Maybe this is a cabin in the woods or maybe it's a hidden storage container that you have buried on some rural property that you own. This second type of cache should have the types of items that you'll need to survive for a longer period of time. The idea is to stay at this location and survive until order can be returned to the town where your home is located.

You may be thinking that there's no way you can afford to stock both your home and your bug out location with all the things you'll need to survive doomsday. If you are, you're not alone. Let's face it: not everyone can afford to purchase a piece of rural land to keep on hand as a bug out location.

One possible solution to this problem is to have what preppers call a "bug out trailer." The idea here is that if you determine that things are beginning to be unsafe where you are bugging in, you can load your bug out trailer with the most essential supplies and take them with you to your long-term bug out location.

This could be to some remote land that you own or it could be to some remote public land. If you don't have the luxury of bugging out on land that you own, the next best thing would be to have a predetermined place in the woods that is on public land as your planned bug out location. The important thing is that you have some plan in place to get your family to a safer location that is far away from those with bad intentions.

Once you arrive at your long-term bug out location, you'll be far away from the hordes of people who intend to do you harm and take what is yours. If you've prepared properly, you'll have the items you'll need to survive at your bug out location and you can wait for things to cool off while keeping your family safe. (For more information about bugging out, see Section 2.)

Be Prepared To Seal Your Windows and Doors

Many people who are into prepping believe that the very cause of doomsday will be some form of chemical warfare such as a dirty bomb. Others believe that a pandemic virus will bring doomsday upon us. Regardless of which group is right, one thing is for sure: All preppers should have enough plastic sheeting and duct tape on hand to seal their doors and windows.

Plastic sheeting can be purchased inexpensively at most major hardware stores. When you go shopping, you'll find  it located in the paint department. What you're looking for are the large plastic drop cloths that painters put down to protect the carpeting while they are painting. This plastic sheeting comes in very large rolls, which makes storing large quantities of it quite easy. It's much cheaper to buy these large plastic drop cloths than it is to buy smaller pieces of plastic window insulation.

During a major event that calls for protecting the air in your home, you can cut this sheeting into pieces that are just big enough to cover your doors and windows. Then, you can use the duct tape that you have stocked away to attach the plastic to the perimeter edges of your doors and windows.

Keeping Things in Perspective When It Comes To Prepping

After reading this book, you may be thinking that there are so many things to prepare for that you'll never be able to get it all done. The most important thing to keep in mind is that even the most diligent preppers never really feel like they have prepared well enough. This goes hand in hand with the very nature of being a prepper. Preppers are constantly thinking ahead and planning for what might happen in the future.

Instead of letting yourself become overwhelmed to the point that it paralyzes you into not doing anything at all to prepare, start eating that elephant one bite at a time and get started prepping today. Make yourself a list of the items that you want to include in your emergency supplies cache and little by little start chipping away at the list. If you are diligent and you stick with it, before long you'll look at everything that you've managed to accumulate and wonder how on earth you were able to do it.

If you don't think that you'll ever be able to stock up on everything that you want to put in your emergency storage, think about the last time you moved. Chances are that as you were packing everything into boxes and loading it into the moving truck, you were amazed at all the junk you had collected over the years. You didn't realize it at the time, but because you were acquiring this junk a little bit at a time, you were able to accumulate much more than you probably realized you had. This same phenomenon is what will help you reach your prepping goals.

Start prepping today with a good plan in place and, before you know it, you'll be ready for doomsday!

SECTION 2

Build the Ideal Bug Out Bag

Introduction

Whether you want to believe it or not, the day may come when you'll have to grab what you can carry and leave your home in a hurry. If you're prepared for this day to come, you'll be much better off than if you simply start grabbing armfuls of items and stuffing them into a suitcase or backpack.

In this section of the book, we'll review what you've already briefly learned about bugging out. Then, we'll teach you more about it, including what it means to bug out, when the right time to bug out is, and how to prepare your family for this very important day. You'll also learn—in detail—how to pack and prepare a bug out bag, which will help this experience go as smoothly as possible. The goal of this author is to provide you with the knowledge that you'll need so that you can prepare a bug out bag that will allow you to thrive and not merely survive if you ever actually have to bug out.

If you're wondering if this book is worth reading, ask yourself this: If you only had five minutes to grab everything that you would need to survive for a period of seventy-two hours and stuff it in a bag, what would you choose to take with you? Most of you would probably be able to think of a few things that are very important to you, such as medications and first-aid supplies, but not many of you would know what you would really need to survive. Even if you did know what to take, unless you take the steps to prepare your bug out bag that will be outlined in this book, you probably wouldn't have the items that you'd need to survive on hand and readily available.

This book will teach you what you need to do today to prepare yourself to survive tomorrow, and to do so without being too uncomfortable!

What the Heck Is Bugging Out Anyway?

While it might sound like bugging out means going crazy, nothing could be further from the truth. As we discussed in Section 1, the term "bugging out" is one that is used by people who spend their time preparing to survive any number of emergencies or natural disasters that our world will likely face in the months or years to come.

When a prepper says that it's time to bug out, he or she means that it's time to leave home and travel to someplace safer. There could be any number of reasons that would necessitate leaving one's home in a hurry and bugging out.

For example, let's imagine that a natural disaster were to take place, such as an earthquake or a hurricane. If the destruction were great enough, your home or apartment building may no longer be structurally safe to occupy. These types of natural events may leave gas lines severed, which may result in natural gas leaks that could create a very dangerous situation for you and your family. Keep in mind that when a natural disaster of this magnitude hits, you may only have minutes to react!

What you do during those first few minutes will play an important role in how smoothly your evacuation goes, as well as how comfortable you and your family will be while you are trying to survive a bug out scenario.

When Should You Bug Out?

Now, let's imagine another scenario that might justify bugging out. Imagine that something were to happen in the town where you live that results in civil unrest, rioting, looting, and marauding. This isn't really too far-fetched if you think about it. As a matter of fact, this kind of scenario unfolds in cities all around the world quite often.

For the purpose of this example, we'll stick to the natural disaster scenario. Imagine that a devastating earthquake were to hit the city where you live. Of course, there would be a tremendous amount of physical damage to the city's infrastructure and buildings, but that's not the most serious threat that you might find yourself facing. The earthquake itself is the immediate threat, but once the ground stops shaking, the very people who occupy the city may become a threat to the safety of you and your family.

History has proven to us time and time again that serious natural disasters tend to bring out the worst in people. The first natural reaction of people is to realize that they don't have the necessary supplies to survive the disaster. This usually results in a flood of people hitting the stores and gas stations in an effort to buy or steal the things they'll need to weather the storm. It's this widespread panic to prepare after the event that brings out the worst in people. When people start to realize that their children will be going hungry in a few hours, they panic! People who would normally be decent, law-abiding citizens will pillage and plunder in an unmerciful fashion to get what they think they'll need to survive. They'll even resort to violence against you and your family to get what they need if they think that you have it.

When faced with looting and marauding invaders, the safest thing for you to do may be to grab your bug out bag and retreat to a safer location. Only you can decide if the situation warrants bugging out since every situation will be unique. That being said, hopefully you'll be prepared to bug out after reading this section and doing the things that it suggests.

Review: What Is a Bug Out Bag?

A bug out bag is simply a backpack or some other type of bag that is stocked with enough emergency supplies for one person to survive for a short period of time. Most experts suggest that you should have enough supplies in your bug out bag to survive for a minimum of seventy-two hours. This is generally considered enough time for emergency services to set up temporary relief outposts that can provide food, shelter, and medical supplies to those who have been displaced by a disaster.

Instead of the term "bug out bag," you may be more familiar with the term "seventy-two-hour kit." The first term is one that is popular amongst preppers, but you may not have heard the term before if you haven't frequented prepping circles or don't have other prepper friends. Regardless of what you choose to call this bag, it's simply some kind of a bag that contains food, medical, and other supplies that you will need to survive for the period of about seventy-two hours.

Selecting the Best Type of Bug Out Bag

Okay, now that you have a basic understanding of what bugging out is, as well as what a bug out bag is, it's time to talk about selecting the best type of bag to fill with your survival supplies. This could be a suitcase, a backpack, a fanny pack, or maybe even a duffle bag. Each of these bags will be capable of holding some of the types of supplies that you'll want to have on hand when you bug out, but one is much more versatile than the others.

The important thing to keep in mind is that if you find yourself needing to bug out, having any kind of bug out bag is better than not having one at all. That being said, remember that if you ever have to actually bug out, you may have to carry your bag for quite some time. With this idea in mind, it's easy to see that a good-quality backpack (that fits you well) is most likely the best type of bag to use.

The primary reason for this is that backpacks are designed to be easily carried while evenly distributing the weight of their contents across your shoulders. Other types of bags will do a fine job of holding your emergency supplies, but if you've ever tried to carry a suitcase with one hand for any length of time, you know how tiring this can be. These types of bags are difficult to carry for very long because you can only use one arm at a time. All of the bag's weight is left hanging from one arm and, not only does this throw your balance off, but your hand and fingers will tire quickly, as well.

If you are to have to carry your seventy-two-hour kit for any length of time, you're going to want to carry one that is designed to be easily carried. For most people, this will be a quality backpack. Some would argue that a suitcase with large wheels could be rolled easier than a backpack could be carried. The problem with this argument is that you can't predict the type of ground you'll need to pull the suitcase across. If the surface is mud or snow, the wheels of the suitcase will likely have a difficult time rolling and you'll be left trying to carry the suitcase with one arm.

Most experts would probably agree that a backpack is the most versatile platform for building a bug out bag, but care must be taken to select the right kind of backpack for the person carrying it. A man who is 6' 4" tall and weighs 200 pounds will physically be able to carry a much larger backpack than a ten-year-old girl can carry. Not only that, an adult will likely be carrying more survival gear than a child. It's important for each member of your family to have a bug out bag, but it's not realistic to expect a young child to carry the same types of things that a grown man will carry.

Remember, each member of your family should have a bug out bag packed and ready to grab at a moment's notice. Because each member of your family is going to be different, you should think about them in terms of their individuality when you are buying a backpack to use for bugging out. Make sure that the backpack you choose fits the person who will be carrying it. Bigger is not always better when it comes to choosing a backpack. After all, what good will the finished bug out bag be if it's too big and heavy for your child or wife to carry?

When it comes to selecting a backpack, you want to keep quality in mind without going overboard. Remember, you won't be climbing Mt. Everest with this bag. Instead you'll be making your way to a safe place to wait out the chaos. You want to buy a backpack that is of good enough quality to hold up; however, you don't need to buy a state-of-the-art $800 carbon fiber backpack either.

Don't lose sight of the fact that this isn't going to be a backpack that you're going to be carrying every day. It's going to be packed and waiting for the day when you may eventually need to grab it and run. Aside from the occasional bug out drill that you might practice with your family, this backpack won't actually be carried very often at all.

That being said, when you do have to carry it, you're going to want to make sure that it's comfortable and properly adjusted. As a general rule, the more gear you plan on carrying in your pack, the higher quality it should be. If you are a big strong man and you plan on carrying extra supplies in your bag, it probably makes sense to purchase a backpack that is designed to carry more weight over longer distances. These types of packs will most likely have a built-in frame as well as a waist belt to help distribute the weight over your body more evenly.

When you are picking a backpack for children to carry, it's probably best to stay away from the packs that only have one shoulder strap. These bags are fashionable but they aren't really designed to evenly distribute weight. Additionally, when choosing a pack for young children to carry, a high-end pack with an internal frame is probably going a bit overboard. A more appropriate pack might be what is commonly called a "day pack."

Keep in mind that as your children grow, so too must their bug out bags. It wouldn't make much sense to pack a bug out bag for your child when he or she is six years old and expect them to carry the same pack when they are sixteen. As they grow and are able to carry a larger pack that will accommodate more supplies, be sure and upgrade their pack accordingly.

To sum things up when it comes to choosing bug out bags, this author suggests that you purchase quality backpacks and that each pack be appropriate for the person carrying it. The members of your family will be different ages and sizes so it's important to have them all try their packs on with the straps adjusted properly before you buy them.

Child Bug Out Bags vs. Adult Bug Out Bags

As responsible parents, you bear the burden of doing all that you can to keep your children safe from harm. When it comes to packing a bug out bag for children, you will need to use your best judgment as to whether you feel like your child is mature enough to safely handle and use any particular items that you include in his or her pack.

As the author, I've tried to include warnings in this book about particular items that might pose a safety hazard to children. I've included these warnings in the spirit of trying to get you thinking about child safety when it comes to packing a bug out bag for your child. Although I've done my best to include any warnings that I could possibly think of, you alone bear the burden and responsibility of making sure that you don't pack items in their bug out bags that may harm your children.

Keep in mind that while bug out bags are designed to store the items one will need to survive, your responsibility as a parent doesn't go away during a survival situation. Many of the items suggested in this book should only be used or handled by adults. Before you pack any item in your child's bug out pack ask yourself if you feel comfortable with him or her having access to the item. If the answer is no, don't put the particular item in his or her pack.

That being said, you may have to bear the burden of carrying extra items in your own pack to aid in the survival of both yourself and your children. When choosing a backpack for a child to carry, keep in mind that children aren't fully developed and consequently, they aren't physically able to carry as much weight as an adult. With this in mind, you will likely have to carry certain items that your child will need to survive in your own backpack.

Another option is to divide the items that your young children aren't physically able to carry between other more mature family members. Remember, if you have to bug out as a family, you'll be surviving as a family. This may mean that the older and stronger members of your family will have to step up to the plate and share the responsibility of carrying some of the items that your youngest children aren't able to. Surviving while bugging out is a team effort and it will take all the members of your team (family) working in harmony to survive together until order can be restored and you can return to your regular routine.

An adult's bug out backpack should be more robust and feature-rich than a child's pack. It should be the type of pack that a backpacker might use on a multiday backpacking trip. These packs will have either an internal or external frame that will serve to help support the load you are carrying as well as provide places to secure extra items to the pack. An adult's pack will also be equipped with more pockets and tie downs for storing extra items. Because you, as an adult, will be carrying many items that your children will need to survive, it makes sense that you'll need a more sophisticated backpack. This of course means that it will cost you more than a child's pack. That being said, you can often find suitable packs at a significant discount at secondhand stores, outlet stores, and even yard sales.

When it comes to choosing a pack for a child to carry, you'll have to use your best judgment about what they are realistically capable of carrying on their back. Young children may only be able to carry the type of backpack that they are typically accustomed to using for their school supplies. The older your child is, the better the chance he or she will be to carry a larger pack. For example, teenagers can probably carry larger packs than young children. You'll have to use your best judgment and choose a pack that is age appropriate for each of the members of your family.

The main thing to remember is that bug out bags aren't any good for your children if they're too big and heavy for them to actually carry. Likewise, a bug out backpack that is too small or poorly constructed won't be able to carry all of the items that you as an adult will need.

What to Include In Your Bug Out Bag

It's important to understand that packing a bug out bag is a very personal thing. Some items are going to be absolutely critical to your survival, while others will simply serve to make life a bit more comfortable for you. This book is going to provide some suggestions about what you might choose to include in your personal survival kit, but they are merely suggestions. You, and you alone, will be responsible for making sure that you pack the right types of items that you need to survive.

Your first priority when it comes to packing a bug out bag is survival. With survival in mind, think about the things that you *can't* live without. This doesn't include your laptop or tablet computer, either. We know that water and food are essential to everyone's survival, but your particular situation may be different than another person's situation. For example, you may require a certain type and amount of prescription medication to survive for three days that someone else doesn't need. You may also have certain food allergies that will need to be taken into consideration when preparing a bug out bag.

Let's first review the basic necessities that you'll need to survive. As we've previously discussed, FEMA lists water, food, and clean air at the top of their list of items to include in a seventy-two-hour survival kit. Everyone, regardless of their personal situation, requires these three things to survive. Consequently, it makes sense to talk about these items first.

Water

As you may remember, in a document written on the subject of emergency preparedness, FEMA says that a normally active person needs a minimum of one half gallon of clean water per day just for drinking. They go on to say that each person should have another half gallon per day to use for sanitation purposes.

Keep in mind that when preparing a bug out bag, someone is going to have to carry it. Young children may not be able to carry this much water themselves, which may mean that as the responsible parent, you may need to carry some of your children's share of water.

This doesn't mean that they shouldn't have water in their survival kit. They absolutely should! You would hope that they never become separated from you, but if something were to cause you to become separated, they will need to have enough water in their bug out bag to survive.

The author of this book prefers to pack commercially bottled water for a couple of reasons. The first is that bottled water is treated to last without spoiling and the second is that once the bottles are used, the empty bottles become convenient containers that can be used for other survival purposes.

Important Note about Water: There are stories that survival experts tell about people dying of dehydration when they actually have water with them. What the experts believe is happening is that people are so concerned with conserving their water rations that they don't drink enough and, consequently, they end up dying of dehydration. Because of these stories, many survivalists use a saying that goes, "Water is better in you than on you." This basically means that you should drink your daily water ration instead of trying to conserve it. Having water on you will do nothing at all to fend off dehydration, while having it inside you will definitely help.

Food

Depending on your size, age, and activity level, your daily food requirements will vary. That being said, you'll need to pack enough food to sustain the person who is carrying the bug out bag for three days. As you can imagine, this creates the question: What kind of food should you pack?

Since you never know when you'll have to grab your bug out bag and run, whatever you pack should be non-perishable and lightweight. Remember, *you* have to carry what you pack, so if your backpack is stuffed with big cans of beef stew, you're going to be pretty miserable if you have to carry your bug out bag very far.

Perhaps a better solution would be to pack a product like the ER Emergency Ration 3600 Survival Food Bar found at www.quakekare.com or 1-800-2-PREPARE.

The manufacturers of this product advertise on their packaging that it is approved by the United States Coast Guard as well as the U.S. Department of Homeland Security. Each 27 oz. packet contains 9 individual 410-calorie food ration bars. This equals a total of 3,690 calories that are all wrapped up in a convenient little package.

You don't need to add water to it and you don't need to cook it. You just open a package and eat it. This product is marketed as a three-day food ration package. Divided over three days, these emergency ration bars will provide 1,230 calories per day. Because of their small size, you can easily pack two emergency ration packages, which will provide

ER Emergency Ration 3600 Survival Food Bar. Photo courtesy: Quakekare.com.

extra calories to fend off hunger. Their small size also means that you should have enough room to pack some comfort foods, such as candy. Having access to these comfort foods will make surviving more tolerable—especially for children.

People seem to have a difficult time deciding what foods to pack in a bug out bag. Products like this emergency ration bar may not be on par with a steak dinner, but they're cheap ($4.09 on Amazon.com), they don't take up much space, they have a five-year shelf life, and they're energy dense. They also come in a vacuum-sealed bag to keep the product neatly packed away and fresh for when you need to eat it. They may not exactly be gourmet, but they will provide you with enough calories to survive. We'll talk about having access to comfort foods, which will make surviving easier, later on in this book.

Clean Air

Some preppers go all out and carry high-end gas masks to ensure that they will have clean air to breathe after a disaster hits. Whether you choose to go to that extent will be up to you. At the very least, you should probably pack some dust masks, cotton shirts, or bandanas that can be used to help filter the air that you'll be breathing. You may not need to use this item, but you'll be glad that you have it if the air quality is in fact poor and you have to bug out.

Medications

A three-day supply of any medications that you need to take should be kept in your bug out bag, as well. If your medications require refrigeration, you may want to check with your doctor and tell him or her that you are preparing a bug out bag. He or she may be able to give you some samples of medications that don't require refrigeration to get you through the seventy-two-hour time period. This is something that you'll have to figure out with your doctor's help.

Warning: Medication can be dangerous if not taken properly. You should use your own discretion as to whether or not to pack it in your children's bug out bags.

Only you know whether your children are mature enough to have their medications packed in their own bags. You may prefer to pack it in your bag and dispense it to them at the appropriate time under your direct supervision.

Infant Supplies

If you'll be caring for an infant that requires infant formula, don't forget to pack enough formula and diapering supplies to last for three days. You'll also need to plan accordingly and make sure that you pack enough extra water to mix the formula for each feeding. Be sure and check to see if the formula you are packing is actually supposed to be mixed with water, as some infant formula is already premixed.

The same holds true if you'll be caring for a toddler that needs to eat canned baby food. You'll be able to survive just fine on emergency ration bars and candy, but your young toddlers may not do so well on this kind of food. Since toddlers can't be expected to carry their own bug out bags, you'll be responsible for carrying the supplies that they'll need to survive so be sure and plan accordingly.

Important Family Documents

You should probably also carry copies of any important family documents that you think might be of use to you. These documents should be stored in a waterproof bag so they don't get ruined if you find yourself having to survive in less than ideal weather conditions. Some examples of the types of documents that you might want to carry are:

1) Photo identification.

2) Important medical information, such as medical history, medical conditions, allergies, or the medications that you might take.

3) Copies of insurance policies or medical insurance cards.

4) Important contact information, including phone numbers and addresses of relatives, close friends, and family doctors.

5) Bank account information.

6) Accurate location of your strategically hidden bug out caches as well as directions to them. This might include GPS coordinates or perhaps even maps with the location of the caches clearly marked on them.

Protection from the Elements

Depending on where you live, you may find yourself having to deal with cold weather when you bug out. Hypothermia is a very real risk in cold climates and it's nothing to take lightly. Simply put, if you're not prepared for the cold, it can kill you.

With this in mind, you should pack at least one change of warm clothing, including a coat or jacket, a long sleeve shirt, long pants, warm shoes or boots, gloves, socks, and a hat. Additionally, each person should have a sleeping bag or warm blanket in his or her survival kit.

While we're on the subject of blankets, now would be a good time to address survival blankets. More specifically, the tightly folded mylar blankets that look like huge sheets of aluminum foil. These emergency blankets, sometimes referred to as "space blankets," should be packed in addition to—not in place of—a sleeping bag or warm blanket. They can be used for a multitude of things including reflecting body heat back toward a person who is wrapped up in the emergency blanket. They can also be used as a reflective surface that may be useful when signaling for help. Again, you probably shouldn't rely on these blankets as your only means of keeping warm, but they are useful items to have on hand and they won't take up much space in your bug out bag, either.

Warning: This item can be dangerous for small children because it may pose a suffocation hazard. Mylar space blankets are not permeable and, if placed over the mouth and nose of a child, the child may suffocate. You should use your own discretion as to whether you are comfortable packing this item in your children's bug out bags. Only you know whether your child is mature enough to safely use this item. If you choose to let your children use this item, it should only be under your direct supervision.

Spending the night in a warm sleeping bag can make the difference between a restful night's sleep and a miserable one. A good sleeping bag can be purchased for $50 to $100, and these bags usually come with compression sacks that make packing them down to a small and easy-to-handle size quite simple. One note about buying sleeping bags is to make sure you buy one that is sized appropriately for the person who will be sleeping in it.

Contrary to what you might think, sleeping bags are not one-size-fits-all items. If you're 6' 4" tall, you'll be glad that you thought ahead and bought a sleeping bag that was long enough to fit your entire body. On the flip side of this scenario, small children don't need to have a full-sized adult sleeping bag strapped to their bug out packs either. This will just add to the bulk and weight that they end up having to carry.

Chemical hand warming pouches are also very useful when trying to fend off the cold. Once opened, these little packs produce heat for several hours. They do eventually stop producing heat, but having access to them could provide an extra measure of comfort that you'll really appreciate having. Not to mention, being able to hand these little wonders to your cold children will help put your mind at ease and help take the chill off of them. Because they can help you keep warm, they may do wonders for your morale and sense of well-being while you try to survive.

Warning: Ingesting the contents of the hand warmer can be dangerous. If you choose to let your child use one of these chemical hand warmers, it should only be under your direct supervision.

A small, lightweight tent is also a good thing to have strapped to your bug out pack. You can survive without a tent, but sleeping in one will be more comfortable than sleeping under the stars. Since this book is about remaining comfortable when you have to bug out, the author highly recommends that you pack a tent with your bug out bag. Not only can a tent provide some shelter from the rain and snow, but it will also keep biting flies and mosquitoes off you. It will even keep you a bit warmer at night!

Depending on the number of people that will be bugging out with you, you may have to pack a few tents. It's much easier to have a few people each carry a small dome tent than it is to pack one large cabin-type tent that could accommodate your entire family.

If, however, you are bugging out by yourself, you might want to pack what is called a "bivy sack" in lieu of a tent. A bivy sack is essentially a very small tent that is just big enough to fit your sleeping bag and a few supplies. It will protect your sleeping bag and supplies from the elements as well as keep the mosquitoes off you while still being so small and lightweight that you'll hardly realize you're packing it with you.

Another very useful item to have with you that can help protect you from the elements is a plastic tarp. You can use this item a variety of ways in survival situations. It can be used as a protective barrier to keep your sleeping bag off the damp ground as well as a cover to protect your supplies from rain and snow. In a pinch, it can even be used as a signaling device.

Warning: This item can be dangerous, as it is not permeable and may pose a suffocation hazard if young children get wrapped up in it. If you choose to let your child carry a plastic tarp in their bug out bag, it should only be under your direct supervision.

Footwear

Since you might have to hike for some distance when you bug out, it's important to have the proper type of footwear. For this reason, you might want to consider keeping a good-quality pair of hiking boots next to your bug out bag. Then, if you ever have to bug out, you can ditch your flip-flops and put on your hiking boots before you leave your house.

Keeping your hiking boots with your family's bug out bags has an added benefit. If you have children, you know that they inevitably have a hard time finding both of their shoes when they are looking for them. By storing their hiking boots with their bug out bag, you're taking that risk out of the equation. This can and will save you time when you are trying to bug out in a hurry.

Personal Sanitation Supplies

Items like moist towelettes, toilet paper, hand sanitizer, feminine hygiene products, personal hygiene products, and garbage bags with plastic ties can come in really handy for taking care of everyday hygiene and sanitation needs. These items are easy to overlook when packing a bug out bag, but when you find yourself needing them, you'll be kicking yourself for not having packed them. Whatever you do, don't make that mistake.

Keep in mind, however, that luxury items like makeup kits and hand mirrors will only add to the bulk and weight that a person has to carry. Your teenage daughter may think that she can't live without these items for three whole days, but she'll be better off if she doesn't have to carry the added weight on her back. Also, not carrying these items means that there will be more room for actual survival items in the backpack.

Warning: Garbage bags should not be included in young children's bug out bags because they pose a suffocation hazard. Additionally, young children should not be allowed to play with them.

First-Aid Kit

Oftentimes during emergency situations, people will become injured and require emergency medical care of some sort. If you're equipped with the proper supplies and knowledge to dress and treat wounds, your chances of surviving until you can get professional medical care will increase substantially. Notice that the word "knowledge" was included in this last statement. It's important for each bug out bag to contain a first-aid kit, but if you don't know how to use it, it will be of little use to you.

You may want to pack a book on first aid to refer to, but good old knowledge about performing first aid is

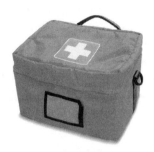

something that doesn't take up any space at all in your bug out bag—and it's something that everyone should have. It's highly advisable that you take the time as soon as possible to get some first-aid training. Be sure to include your entire family in this training. After all, you never know when the knowledge that your family has may end up saving *your* life.

Warning: Some items that are included in first-aid kits could potentially be dangerous if handled by young children. You should inspect the first-aid kits that you pack in your children's bug out bags to make sure that there aren't any items in the kit that may harm them.

Multitool

As we discussed in Section 1, a multitool can be invaluable to have on hand. It can be used as a wrench to help you turn off utilities, as a knife to use for cutting, and much more. You may remember that there are a lot of cheap knockoffs on the market when it comes to multitools. It has been the experience of the author that it's worth spending the money on a high-quality name brand multitool. They're built much better than cheaper versions and the added quality that they bring to the table may be the difference between them saving your bacon and being a worthless pile of junk.

 It's also worth pointing out that when you are buying a multitool, you are in fact buying a *tool* that will be used. With this in mind, the cute little keychain-sized multitools should probably be avoided—they aren't equipped to handle the same types of jobs as good-quality, regular-sized multitools.

Warning: This item can be dangerous because multitools are usually equipped with a knife blade. You should use your own discretion as to whether to pack it in your children's bug out bags. Only you know whether your child is mature enough to safely use this tool.

Survival Knife

Depending on the climate and the time of year that you find yourself bugging out, you may have to build shelter or light a fire. A good-quality survival knife that is substantial enough to be used for the tasks of cutting limbs or chopping wood can be very useful in this type of a situation. This author likes the Gerber Gator Machete Jr. for this purpose. It's a large, double-edged knife that has a chopping edge as well as a good-quality saw on the back edge. It has a 10.75" blade and measures a total of 18.75" in length. It's a good hacking and sawing tool that comes with a sheath and will only set you back about $25 or $30.

Warning: This tool is potentially dangerous and should not be packed in a child's bug out bag. Additionally, it should only be used by an adult.

Fire Starting Kit

A good-quality fire starting kit is essential for any adult's bug out bag. Be sure and include items that will make it easy for you to start a fire. Even if you know how to make a fire with a fire bow, you'll be glad that you thought ahead and packed items like a high-quality magnesium stick, a new butane lighter, waterproof matches, and dry tinder. Being able to start a fire—and quickly—can save your life during extreme, cold survival situations. It can provide heat, light, protection from biting insects, a way of signaling for help, and even protection from predatory animals. Not to mention, fire is a great comforter when a person is in a survival situation.

Here's a helpful tip! If you pack a new butane lighter in a hard plastic container that is used for holding a travel toothbrush, the lever that releases the gas on the lighter won't accidentally be depressed when you pack it in your bug out pack. If you don't pack it this way and the lever does accidentally become depressed while the lighter is being jostled around in your pack, all of the gas could escape and the lighter will be of little use to you when you actually need to use it.

Warning: Starting a fire can be dangerous, as there is potential of suffering burns or other injuries. You should use your own discretion as to whether to pack fire starting tools in your children's bug out bags. Only you know whether your child is mature enough to safely use them.

Emergency Radio

An emergency radio with NOAA weather radio frequencies preprogrammed and a tone alert can be invaluable to you and your family during a bug out situation. You can purchase emergency radios that will sound a tone to alert you to important messages from officials. Ideally, the emergency radio that you keep in your bug out bag will be both battery-powered and operable via a hand crank. Be sure to pack an extra set or two of batteries so that you can keep the radio on nearly all the time. This is where the hand crank feature comes in handy. Every so often, you can wind the crank on the radio to charge the internal battery. You never know when that important emergency message will be broadcasted, and you don't want to miss hearing it, so be sure and do all you can to keep the radio on and monitored at all times.

 Here's something that's worth remembering: Having little chores to do like winding the radio or listening for emergency broadcasts can help keep children from worrying too much during a stressful situation that has forced you to bug out with your family.

Emergency Flashlight

Remember—a flashlight can be an invaluable tool to have in your pack. It can be used to help you do chores and find items during the long dark nights as well as for signaling should you need to attract the attention of rescuers. When shopping for a flashlight to include in your bug out bag, choose one that has an LED bulb. LED bulbs are very energy efficient and they'll make your batteries last much longer than the old-fashioned incandescent bulbs. If your flashlight uses batteries, be sure and pack extra batteries in your bug out bag.

 As we've discussed, many flashlights that are designed for emergency use have a hand crank charging feature. This is a good feature to have since you never have to worry about the batteries dying. When the charge runs out, a few minutes of turning the crank will get you back in business. Another good feature to look for in an emergency flashlight is a signaling setting. Some emergency flashlights can be switched to signal mode, which causes them to flash on and off every few seconds. Some even have a red flashing light to do an even better job of attracting the attention of rescuers.

Signaling Whistle

You may find yourself in a situation where you must find a way to attract the attention of potential rescuers.

 We've already talked about using a mylar emergency blanket, a plastic tarp, and a flashlight as signaling devices, but it's important to have a good signaling whistle in your bug out bag, too. Search and rescue personnel have reported that it's much easier for them to hear a whistle than a person's voice. The sound of a whistle will carry much farther than a voice. Not only that, after a person has been calling for help for quite some time, their voice becomes frail to the point that it is very difficult, if not impossible, for potential rescuers to hear.

Signal Flare

A signal flare or a flare gun can help you get the attention of would-be rescuers, as well. When emergency personnel are searching for people in need of help, they may only have a brief window of time to pinpoint your location. A perfect example of this might be if rescue personnel are flying over you in search planes. Having a signal flare may be the difference between whether they see you or pass right by you.

Warning: This item can be dangerous and it should never be packed in a child's bug out bag. Additionally, it should only be used by an adult or under the direct supervision of an adult.

Emergency Rain Poncho

Since you can't predict what the weather conditions will be if you ever have to bug out, it's a good idea to pack an emergency rain poncho in your seventy-two-hour kit. This item is small, inexpensive, and easy to pack. You may not need to use it, but you'll be glad that you have it if you do end up spending much time in the rain.

Warning: This item can be dangerous for small children because it may pose a suffocation hazard. Plastic rain ponchos are not permeable and if placed over the mouth and nose of a child, they may suffocate. You should use your own discretion as to whether you are comfortable packing this item in your children's bug out bags. Only you know whether your child is mature enough to safely use this item. If you choose to let your children use this item, it should only be under your direct supervision.

Household Chlorine Bleach

A small quantity of regular household chlorine bleach can be used to disinfect things when it is diluted at a ratio of nine parts water to one part bleach. You can also use it to treat water in an emergency: use sixteen drops of bleach per one gallon of water.

Warning: Don't use scented bleach, colorsafe bleach, or bleach with added cleaners. This item should only be packed in the bug out bags of adults. Additionally, it should only be used by an adult or under the direct supervision of an adult.

Cordage

Each adult's bug out pack should have some rope bundled in it. This can be used for everything from building a shelter to making a solar still for distilling water. The list of uses for rope and cords is virtually endless in a survival situation. Many survival experts prefer to pack 550 paracord. This cordage is lightweight and strong, and you can pull the inner strands out to have access to lighter-weight cordage if you want to.

Warning: This item can be dangerous for small children because it may pose a strangulation hazard. Only you know whether your child is mature enough to safely use this item. If you choose to let your children use this item, it should only be under your direct supervision.

Pet Supplies

Many families have at least one pet, which means that some thought and consideration should be given to the survival needs of pets, too. If you plan on bugging out, you should be prepared to grab the family dog or cat and take them with you. This means that you'll have to plan accordingly for their food and water needs, as well. One idea is to train your dog to carry a pet backpack. You can find these backpacks at most quality pet stores and, once your dog has been trained to carry one, it can help lighten your load by carrying its own food supply.

You also want to make sure that you have some way of keeping your pet contained. If you have a cat, this likely means that you'll bug out with a cat carrier. If you have

a dog, this will likely mean that you'll pack a leash so that you can keep your dog tied up. Keeping your pets contained or tied up is not only for your convenience, but it could also save their lives. If emergency vehicles are blaring their horns and sirens, your pets may panic and run off, causing them to get lost, or worse, killed by a passing vehicle.

Money

You never know when having some money available to you may come in handy. You may be able to pay someone for help or you may need to purchase something from a store or from someone. Keep in mind that whatever denomination of currency that you have on hand is the amount you're going to have to pay. For example, if you only have a $100 bill and you need to buy something like matches from someone, there's a good chance that they won't have $95 dollars on them to make change for you. This means that if you really want the matches, you're going to have to pay $100. With this in mind you should probably keep a supply of small bills on hand. As an interesting note, FEMA suggests that you keep cash, traveler's checks, and change in your bug out bag.

Paper and Pencil

You may receive information from relief personnel that you'll want to write down. Each bug out bag should be equipped with some paper and a pencil just for this purpose. You might want to consider keeping it stored in the watertight bag where your important documents are also stored.

Navigation Aids

You may find yourself having to navigate your way to a particular location during a natural disaster that has caused you to bug out. Having a good set of maps of your area, a compass, and possibly even a handheld GPS could come in handy.

When it comes to the map and compass, they won't be of much use to you unless you know how to use them. Along with preparing by physically packing the items you might need while bugging out, you can prepare by learning how to use a map and compass ahead of time. The time you develop orienteering skills should not be the first time you take your compass out of its package.

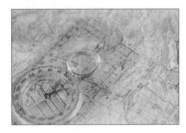 Likewise, if you're going to keep a GPS in your bug out bag, you should take the time to preprogram key waypoints into it ahead of time. Having waypoints like your bug out site,

bug out caches, water sources, etc., preprogrammed into the GPS could really be advantageous when you are in a survival situation. It should go without saying that a stressful real-life survival situation is not the time to try and learn how to use your fancy new GPS. Any time spent learning how to navigate with your GPS ahead of time will be time well spent.

Duct Tape

Many people will tell you that you can fix just about anything with duct tape. This is a bit of an exaggeration, but nonetheless duct tape has many uses in a survival situation. It comes in huge rolls, but many survivalists save space in their packs by buying smaller rolls. They then peel the cardboard out of the inside of the roll and flatten the roll in a vice. This can make packing a roll of duct tape in a bug out bag a little more convenient.

Comfort Items

This is especially important if you're packing a bug out bag for your young children. If you have to suddenly leave your home and try to survive in a camp or some other unfamiliar location, having some comfort items like a coloring book, a stuffed animal, a puzzle book, or some small toys can really help alleviate any stress that your child may be feeling. For those of you who are more mature, a paperback novel might be a good thing to pack to help pass the time and lighten the mood of the situation.

Feel Free to Be Creative When Packing

If you've done a good job picking your emergency supplies, there may be room for additional items in your bug out bag. Remember that the items listed previously are the basic survival items that the author of this book feels are important to pack. That being said, the author won't be with you when you have to bug out, so if you think that you should have some additional items in your bug out backpack, by all means, feel free to pack them.

One word of caution is to try and not over pack. Survivalists have to balance what they think they'll need during a survival situation with what they would like to have. If you're not careful, it's easy to get carried away and pack much more than you'll actually need. There's an old saying that goes, "One can never be too prepared." Well, that may be true, but if you go overboard while packing your bug out bag, you may find yourself having to ditch some of the items along the way so that your pack is light enough to actually carry.

A better solution would be to store luxury items and extra survival items in strategically hidden "bug out caches." We've discussed this earlier in the book, but will talk about it in more detail later.

How to Pack Your Bug Out Bag

Another reason that the author recommends using a backpack as the platform to carry your bug out supplies is the versatility they provide when it comes to packing and organizing things. Most high-quality packs will have the ability to lash several items to the outside of them. Items like sleeping bags, tents, and tarps should be tightly rolled and securely tied to the outer frame of the pack. Note that some packs have internal frames, but many of these types of packs still have places to lash these big and bulky items to.

The more securely these items are tied to your pack, the easier it will be to carry. One tip to remember when packing a bug out bag is that loosely packed items can shift around inside of your pack, causing its center of gravity to constantly change. This constant shifting of weight will make carrying your bug out pack very uncomfortable.

Instead of simply stuffing loose clothing into your pack, consider rolling each item tightly and securing it with strips of electrical tape. This will help compact these items and make it easier to find homes for them in your backpack.

Remember, you're going to pack your bug out bag and it may be several months before you look inside it again. This means that there's a very high likelihood that you'll forget where you packed the individual items. Instead of having to dig through all of the pockets in your pack to find a particular item, consider making a "pack map." This is simply a piece of paper that has an inventory of all the items that your bug out bag contains, along with which pocket they are each packed into. Keep this little pack map in the most easily accessible pocket of your pack and it can save you a lot of time and frustration when you need to find an emergency item in a hurry.

As a general rule, you're going to want to pack the things that you'll need to access the most often in the easiest to access pockets. For example, you don't want to have to dig through your entire pack just to get a drink of water. On the other hand, supplies like your change of clothes can be packed near the bottom of your pack because you won't need to access them as frequently.

After you pack your backpack, you should try to carry it for a while. This will help you know if you've packed too many heavy items near the top, which may throw your center of balance off and make carrying the backpack quite difficult.

Keeping Your Bug Out Bags Up to Date

If you're being responsible about the way you're packing the bug out bags for your family, you'll be constantly updating them. This is especially true if you have growing children in your family. We've already addressed the issue of upgrading the size and type of pack that your growing children are equipped with, but there's another issue to consider. During times of growth spurts, your children may outgrow their clothing two or three times a year. When you realize that your children require larger clothes, replace the old clothing that you have packed away in their bug out bags with new clothing that fits them properly. This includes their hiking boots.

Some other things that may need to be updated are medical records and medications. Your needs may also change. For example, you might have had a new baby since the last time you updated your bug out bags. Whatever the case may be, it's important that you take a few hours at least a couple of times a year and make sure that if you had to bug out, your bug out bags are up to date and ready to go.

Bug Out Caches Can Be Game Changers

This chapter is really important. In it, you'll learn the secret to bugging out comfortably vs. barely surviving if you ever need to bug out. A "bug out cache" is simply a container that is hidden at your preplanned bug out location or at strategic places along the route to your bug out location. Not many people put enough emphasis on the importance of good bug out caches. They really can be game changers when you are trying to survive! As we said in Section 1, think of them like little minimarts for the survivalist.

A good bug out cache is one that is hidden well, protected from the elements, and well stocked with additional survival supplies. Without a doubt, the heaviest item that you'll be packing in your bug out bag is water. One gallon of water weighs 8.35 pounds. This means that if you're packing three gallons, which is what FEMA advises, you'll have to tote around 25.05 pounds of water per person! Some of your family members may not physically be strong enough to do that. Extra water is perhaps one of the most important items to put in a bug out cache. This doesn't mean that you shouldn't keep water in your bug out packs. It's essential to your very survival that you do! It just means that you'll have the ability to access more clean water that you don't have to pack around on your back if you've taken the time to prepare some well stocked bug out caches.

Real food like canned beef stew or even MREs are also good items to keep stashed away in bug out caches. Sure, you can survive on your emergency ration bars but you'll really appreciate the chance to eat a nice hot meal while you're trying to survive the chaos. Comfort foods like junk food is also a good thing to keep in bug out caches. These items can really alleviate a lot of the stress that the situation might be placing on your children. If you can surprise them with a late night treat of something like warm s'mores, surviving while bugging out will be much more tolerable.

Other things to keep in bug out caches are luxury items that will help pass the time. Books, magazines, puzzles, games, and radios can effectively transform a stressful survival situation into a leisurely camping trip that your family might actually enjoy.

The bottom line is that you absolutely should have several well-stocked bug out caches strategically positioned at your preplanned bug out location(s). You should also keep an accurate record of exactly where they are in your bug out bag with your important documents. After all, they won't be of much use to you if you don't remember where you hid or buried them.

Something that you might not have thought of is making a game of digging up your bug out caches with your young children. With a little creativity and imagination, you can turn this chore into a pirate's adventure of following a treasure map to find your hidden treasure.

Having access to these bug out caches truly means that you'll be able to bug out in style. You can do this because you'll have access to comfort and luxury items to help alleviate the discomfort of being displaced from your home while you are waiting for order to be restored. Their level of importance *cannot* be stressed enough.

Be Prepared to Bug Out Quickly

If a natural disaster or other major event that necessitates bugging out occurs, you may only have a few moments to gather your supplies and leave your home. This means that to make the act of bugging out go as smoothly as possible, you're going to want to make sure that a couple of things are in place.

First, you need to have a dedicated location for storing all bug out bags. If you let your children keep them in their rooms and you have to find their bags quickly, you may find that this is easier said than done. In an emergency, minutes count, so make sure that *all* bug out bags are easily accessible and ready to grab.

Second, you want to have a good bug out plan in place. You need to know where you'll go if you have to leave your home quickly. The time of the emergency is *not* an appropriate time to make this decision. That being said, you should have several bug out routes preplanned. If you plan on leaving the city and taking a particular highway and the disaster has turned that highway into a parking lot, you'll want to have preplanned an alternate evacuation route. If you know where you're going ahead of time, and you have a few alternate routes for how to get there, things will go much smoother for you if you ever actually have to bug out.

Third, you want to make sure that you get in the habit of keeping your vehicle's fuel tanks full. When you leave on vacation, the last thing you probably do before you head out is hit the gas station to fill up your tanks. You may not have this luxury during an emergency bug out situation. Even if the gas stations are open, you can bet that you won't be the only one with this idea and you may find that the gas station is a chaotic mess. In the interest of emergency preparedness, a good habit to develop is to always keep your fuel tanks as full as possible.

You might also want to consider storing a couple of five-gallon gas cans at your house so that if you do have to bug out, you can quickly top off your car's tank with the gas that you have on hand. If you do decide to store gasoline, you should buy fresh gas and add a fuel stabilizing preservative such as STA-BIL to it before you store it. This will prolong the shelf life of the gasoline so that it's as fresh as possible when you need it. It should go without saying that you should never store gasoline indoors!

Lastly, you should practice bugging out with your family. This means that you should do what preppers like to call "bug out drills." Basically, these drills are just like fire drills. They should come at unexpected times to truly test how quickly your family can pick up and leave. You'll want to see how quickly you can grab your bug out bags, how quickly you can get everyone loaded in the car, and how long it takes to get to your planned bug out location.

When you arrive at your bug out location, be sure that you spend some time hiking while carrying your bug out packs. This will help prepare you and your family members for what it might be like when you actually have to bug out. It will also help you figure out if the pack that you purchased is configured properly for you. The only way to know what it will feel like to carry your bug out bag on your back is to actually do it while hiking.

There's no substitute for real-world, in-the-field experience. You just can't experience carrying a bug out bag over distance in your living room. The time to figure out that you need to make weight distribution adjustments or other adjustments to your backpack is during these drills, not during an actual emergency.

If you have young children, you can make a game of these drills. You don't have to use the term "bugging out" with your young children either. Instead you can use terms like "let's go camping" or "let's go on a picnic." If they are used to you surprising them at a moment's notice with a camping trip, a real-life bug out situation won't be as stressful to them.

When you arrive at your bug out location, it's important to practice doing some of the things you would have to do to survive a real emergency scenario. Perhaps the easiest way to accomplish this is to periodically take your family on camping trips. If they are accustomed to camping, going through the motions of surviving a real bug out emergency will be much less traumatic.

The main thing to remember is that you don't want panic to set in if you ever actually have to grab your survival kits and bug out. The more familiar your family is with the act of physically grabbing their bug out bags and getting in the car quickly, the less stressful a real emergency will be for them and the more smoothly your evacuation will go.

Arm Yourself with the Knowledge to Survive

It's a good idea to pack a good survival field guide in your bug out bags. This can be used as a reference to help you survive when you are waiting for help from emergency services. As useful as a good field guide can be, there's no replacement for knowledge.

How can you learn how to bug out properly? The best way is to learn to be a survivor. You can attend survival clinics, read books, spend time camping to develop your survivalist skill set, and more. Preparing to bug out isn't like buying something like a fire extinguisher for your home. When you buy a fire extinguisher, you most likely mount it to the wall and forget about it until you need it. When you need to use it, there's not much skill involved, so using it doesn't require much training.

Depending on where you plan on bugging out with your family, you may need quite a bit of skill to survive. If you plan to bug out at your family cabin, you may think that you don't need much skill or training to survive, but what if the roads are closed and you can't make it to your cabin? You might find yourself having to seek shelter in a totally unfamiliar environment. It's these types of unfamiliar situations that you need training to survive.

If you work in an office and you've never taken your family to a park, let alone camping, the experience of trying to survive when you are bugging out could be quite traumatic. Anything you can do to fill your mind with knowledge AND experiences will raise the likelihood that you'll be prepared to help your family survive a real emergency.

HEED THESE WORDS: Take the time to get survival training and gain knowledge *now* and you'll be glad that you did later!

Summary

Hopefully the day will never come that you will have to bug out and leave the safety and comfort of your home, but if it does, you'll be glad that you read this book. More importantly, you'll be glad that you followed the advice in this book and took the time to prepare well stocked bug out bags!

It's much better to be safe than sorry when it comes to matters of emergency preparedness. If you never need to use your bug out bags, that's great! The odds are, however, that you will at some point in the future. Please take the time now to prepare your bug out bags as well as your mind so that you'll be ready if and when this day ever comes.

Photo Credits

All photos purchased from ShutterStock.com unless otherwise noted.

Page #	Photographer/Author
5	Best3d
7	Yeko Photo Studio
8	Steve Collender
10	Ekkachai
11	alexmillos
13	K. Faraktinov
15	Jacob Kearns
16	Sangoiri
16	Lana Langlois
19	Alison Hancock
20	Anne Kitzman
21	Marek Velechovsky
22	Shane Trotter
26	Thomas Barrat
27	Nikita Chisnikov
29	trekandshoot
31	Razmarinka
32	Ivan Ponomarev
33	Richard Nelson